SCIENTIFIC AMERICAN EXPLORE

# Exploring Mars

The Editors of *Scientific American*

SCIENTIFIC
AMERICAN

EDUCATIONAL
PUBLISHING

New York

Published in 2024 by Scientific American Educational Publishing
in association with **The Rosen Publishing Group**
2544 Clinton Street, Buffalo NY 14224

Contains material from Scientific American®, a division of Springer Nature America, Inc.,
reprinted by permission, as well as original material from The Rosen Publishing Group®.

First Edition

**Scientific American**
Lisa Pallatroni: Project Editor

**Rosen Publishing**
Michael Hessel-Mial: Compiling Editor
Michael Moy: Senior Graphic Designer

Cataloging-in-Publication Data
Names: Scientific American, Inc.
Title: Exploring Mars / edited by the Scientific American Editors
Description: New York : Scientific American Educational Publishing, 2024. |
Series: Scientific American explores big ideas | Includes glossary and index.
Identifiers: ISBN 9781725349544 (pbk.) | ISBN 9781725349551
(library bound)| ISBN 9781725349568 (ebook)
Subjects: LCSH: Mars (Planet).
Classification: LCC QB641.E675 2024 | DDC 523.43–dc23

Manufactured in the United States of America
*Websites listed were live at the time of publication.*

Cover: Gorodenkoff/Shutterstock.com

CPSIA Compliance Information: Batch # SACS24.
For Further Information contact Rosen Publishing at 1-800-237-9932.

# CONTENTS

Introduction     6

## Section 1: Unmanned Mars Missions     7

1.1   Skiing to Mars: The Original Rovers     8
By Caleb A. Scharf

1.2   Mars From Mariner 9     11
By Bruce C. Murray

1.3   The Great Martian Storm of '71     27
By Caleb A. Scharf

1.4   The Mars Pathfinder Mission     30
By Matthew P. Golombek

1.5   A New Way to Reach Mars Safely, Anytime and
on the Cheap     40
By Adam Hadhazy

1.6   China Lands Tianwen-1 Rover on Mars in a Major
First for the Country     45
By Jonathan O'Callaghan

## Section 2: Possible Mars Settlements     49

2.1   Human Missions to Mars Will Look Completely
Different from *The Martian*     50
By Lee Billings

2.2   Is "Protecting" Mars from Contamination a
Half-Baked Idea?     54
By Michael J. Battaglia

2.3   Can Mars Be Terraformed?     58
By Christopher Edwards and Bruce Jakosky

2.4   Aerogel Mars     61
By Caleb A. Scharf

2.5   Surviving Mars     64
By Caleb A. Scharf

2.6   How to Grow Vegetables on Mars     69
By Edward Guinan, Scott Engle, and Alicia Eglin

## Section 3: Searching for Martian Life     73

3.1   Water Flows on Mars Today, NASA Announces     74
By Clara Moskowitz

3.2   Searching for Life in Martian Water Will Be Very, Very Tricky     77
By Lee Billings

3.3   The Search for Life on Mars Is About to Get Weird     81
By Leonard David

3.4   Curiosity Rover Uncovers Long-Sought Organic Materials on Martian Surface     87
By Adam Mann

3.5   Deep within Mars, Liquid Water Offers Hope for Life     92
By Lee Billings

3.6   I'm Convinced We Found Evidence of Life on Mars in the 1970s     97
By Gilbert V. Levin

3.7   Until Recently, People Accepted the "Fact" of Aliens in the Solar System     102
By Caleb A. Scharf

## Section 4: Geology on Mars     106

4.1   The Many Faces of Mars     107
By Philip R. Christensen

4.2   Data Deluge: Texas Flood Canyon Offers Test of Hydrology Theories for Earth and Mars     118
By John Matson

4.3   I Can Tell You about Mars     121
By David Bressan

4.4   Martian Mile-High Mounds Mystery: The Answer Is Blowing in the Wind     124
By Shannon Hall

4.5   Water on Mars May Be Trapped in the Planet's Crust, Not Lost to Space     127
By Jonathan O'Callaghan

## Section 5: The Dynamic Martian Climate     131

5.1   Global Climatic Change on Mars     132
by Jeffrey S. Kargel and Robert G. Strom

5.2   The Distant Shores of Mars     144
By Caleb A. Scharf

5.3   Dust Bowl Mars                                                  147
         By Caleb A. Scharf

5.4   NASA's Curiosity Rover Finds Unexplained
         Oxygen on Mars                                               150
         By Robin George Andrews


Glossary                                                              155

Further Information                                                   157

Citations                                                            158

Index                                                                159

# INTRODUCTION

The story of human understanding of Mars is one of discovery, imagination, changed expectations, and labored research. We've come a long way from the 19th century, which gave us early knowledge of Mars's moons and geography, but also led many to become overenthusiastic about the planet's likelihood of harboring sentient life. We now know the planet is much harsher than we imagined, with its thin atmosphere, toxic soils, heavy radiation, and no magnetic field. And yet, we also have learned that Mars has an abundance of water (some of it even in liquid form), a dynamic climate, and subtle signatures of potential microbe life. This hard-won knowledge is different from what we imagined, but it is real and invites potential learning.

Of course, research on our neighbor planet is also motivated by dreams of visiting in person. Books like *The Martian* imagine growing potatoes in Mars's alien soil, while engineers devise radiation-shielding aerogel and the press releases of private space companies promise Martian cities before decade's end. Not all of these dreams will translate into reality; Mars's dangers might not be surmounted, and we must take seriously the risk of contaminating the planet with our own microbes. But as some of the articles in this book suggest, it is in naming the challenges that our science can begin to overcome them.

The articles in this title document that process of exploration in five distinct sections. The first focuses on unmanned research, from the early orbital observers in the 1960s and 1970s to the sophisticated rovers of present day. The second focuses on changing prospects of human exploration and habitation of Mars, which have become more cautious in light of new evidence. The third documents the newest research on possible Martian life. The fourth section is about Martian geology, which remains active and un-earthlike. The final section on Mars's climate shows that while the planet is harsh and alien, it remains complex and ever-changing.

# Section 1: Unmanned Mars Missions

1.1    Skiing to Mars: The Original Rovers
By Caleb A. Scharf

1.2    Mars From Mariner 9
By Bruce C. Murray

1.3    The Great Martian Storm of '71
By Caleb A. Scharf

1.4    The Mars Pathfinder Mission
By Matthew P. Golombek

1.5    A New Way to Reach Mars Safely, Anytime, and on the Cheap
By Adam Hadhazy

1.6    China Lands Tianwen-1 Rover on Mars in Major First for the Country
By Jonathan O'Callaghan

# Skiing to Mars: The Original Rovers

By Caleb A. Scharf

As the world waits with bated breath for NASA's Curiosity rover to attempt a safe landing on Mars on August 6th (EDT), it's interesting to recall the rovers of times past. We've all heard about Spirit (R.I.P. 2010) and Opportunity (still kicking), and their immediate technological precursor Sojourner (part of the Mars Pathfinder mission), but long before these plucky robots turned their wheels in the martian regolith there was an earlier generation of explorers trying to make their mark.

In 1971 the Soviet Union launched two nearly identical spacecraft towards the red planet; Mars 2 and Mars 3. Each consisted of an orbiter and a lander, with the latter carrying remarkable little machines—the first Mars rovers.

The plan was for the descent modules to enter the martian atmosphere, use their engines and attitude jets to control and slow their motion, and to deploy parachutes before making a fairly hard impact—instruments cushioned only by foam in the nearly spherical landing capsules. Each of these capsules was about four feet across, and together with their aero-braking heat shields and fueled retro rockets they amounted to about 2,500 lbs Earth-weight. On landing the capsules would open 4 "petals" to help right themselves (an approach duplicated by later rover missions) and orientate their instruments.

The special passenger in each was a tiny 10 lb Earth-weight rover, known simply as "Prop-M." A Prop-M rover was attached to the landing capsule by a fifteen-meter umbilical, carrying power and telemetry. The method of locomotion was simple and ingenious; cross-country skiing. Each rover sat on a pair of metal skids, or skis, that would shuffle back and forth to inch the rover forward across Mars. Whoever designed this was clearly familiar with getting around in long snow-covered winters—and given that no-one knew what the surface consistency was on Mars this method of travel made a great deal of sense. It was also mechanically straightforward, barely more than a child's wind-up toy, with little to go wrong.

Except, sadly, surviving the rigors of actually trying to land on another planet. The Mars 2 lander failed due to an over-steep entry angle and became the first piece of human-produced wreckage on Mars. Mars 3 fared somewhat better, achieving a historic soft landing—but transmitting for barely 15 seconds before failing. Had the landings gone better the Prop-M rovers would have been placed on the regolith by a mechanical arm before skiing off. Each had rudimentary obstacle detection mechanisms—simple metal rods that if pushed would cause the rover to turn, and each carried instruments to test for regolith density and penetration depth at regular intervals. The lander capsule itself carried a scanning electronic camera (not unlike that on the later Viking landers) and atmospheric measuring devices (including a mass spectrometer). It also had the ability to examine surface samples for chemistry and constitution—and particularly to test for the presence of organic (carbon) compounds.

Unfortunately the only image transmitted by Mars 3 appears to have consisted of noise. Had the mission lasted for a few minutes more Prop-M could have become the first tourist to be photographed on the surface of Mars. The Soviet scientists also knew that by observing the tracks left by the Prop-M rovers they would learn about the composition of the martian regolith, a trick that was eventually used decades later.

Despite the failures in landing, the Mars 2 and 3 orbiters sent back a wealth of information on the martian environment and topography, a remarkable achievement coming barely 2 years after humans set foot on the Moon.

So on August 6th 2012, as we wait nervously to hear whether Curiosity has made it safely to the interior of Gale Crater, spare a thought for those pioneering rovers that almost managed to ski on Mars more than forty years ago.

*The views expressed are those of the author(s) and are not necessarily those of Scientific American.*

## About the Author

*Caleb A. Scharf is director of astrobiology at Columbia University. He is author and co-author of more than 100 scientific research articles in astronomy and astrophysics. His work has been featured in publications such as* New Scientist, Scientific American, Science News, Cosmos Magazine, Physics Today *and* National Geographic. *For many years he wrote the Life, Unbounded blog for* Scientific American.

# Mars From Mariner 9

By Bruce C. Murray

A little more than a year ago, in November, 1971, the complex robot spacecraft Mariner 9 fired its braking rocket and was captured in orbit around M ars, thus becoming the first man-made satellite of another planet. From its orbital station, ranging between 1,650 and 17,100 kilometers (1,025 and 10,610 miles) above the surface, Mariner 9 started sending back to the earth a steady stream of pictures and scientific information that was to continue for nearly a year. By the time its instruments had been turned off Mariner 9 had provided about 100 times the amount of information accumulated by all previous flights to Mars. It had also decisively changed man's view of the planet that generations of astronomers and fiction writers had thought most closely resembled the earth. As a result of the Mariner 9 mission it is now possible to make plausible conjectures about the geology of Mars, conjectures comparable, say, to those made about the moon in the early 1960s.

It will be recalled that the first closeup pictures of Mars, made in 1965 by Mariner 4, revealed a planetary surface whose principal features were large craters reminiscent of the bleak surface of the moon. Four years later the pictures sent back by Mariner 6 and Mariner 7 showed that the Martian surface was not uniformly cratered but had large areas of chaotic terrain unlike anything ever seen on either the earth or the moon. In addition a vast bowl-shaped area, long known to earthbound astronomers as the "desert" Hellas, turned out to be nearly devoid of features down to the resolving power of the Mariners' cameras. None of the pictures returned by the first three Mariners showed any evidence of volcanic activity, leading to the view that Mars was tectonically inactive.

This view has had to be drastically revised in the light of the photographs sent back by Mariner 9. The new evidence emerged slowly as the clouds of dust that had shrouded the planet for weeks settled. It revealed, among other things, four large volcanic mountains larger than any such volcanic features on the earth. The Mariner 9 pictures also show a vast system of canyons, tributary gullies and sinuous channels that look at first glance as if they had been created by flowing water. Elsewhere on the planet's surface there is no suggestion of water erosion. That is probably the major mystery presented by the highly successful mission of Mariner 9.

Designed and built by the Jet Propulsion Laboratory of the California Institute of Technology, as were the earlier Mariners, Mariner 9 was crammed with instruments and electronic gear. After burning 900 pounds of retro-rocket fuel, which it had transported 287 million miles in 167 days, Mariner 9 weighed 1,350 pounds when it finally went into orbit around Mars. The cameras and instruments it carried were designed by several groups of investigators from government laboratories and more than a score of universities. The television team, to which I belonged, was headed by Harold Masursky of the U .S. Geological Survey and had nearly 30 members. Somewhat smaller groups were responsible for designing and analyzing data from the ultraviolet spectrometer, the infrared radiometer and the infrared interferometric spectrometer. Other groups had the task of analyzing the trajectory data (which have provided information about the gravitational anomalies of Mars) and the data provided by nearly 100 occultations of the spacecraft's radio Signals (which have yielded new knowledge of the planet's atmosphere and surface).

## The Old Mars

There were strong reasons for the traditional belief in the resemblance between Mars and the earth. Mars rotates once every 24½ hours and its axis is tipped from the plane of its orbit by almost exactly the same amount as the axis of the earth, thus providing the same basis for the seasonal changes in the amount of solar radiation received by the planet's two hemispheres. Mars has white polar caps, originally thought to be composed of water, that alternate from one hemisphere to the other once every Martian year (687 Earth days). The planet also exhibits dark and light markings that change on a seasonal basis.

Early astronomers speculated that the dark markings might be vegetation. Later and more cautious workers still found it plausible that Mars had had an early history similar to the earth's, which implied the existence of oceans and an atmosphere with enough water vapor to precipitate and erode the surface. Because of Mars's small mass (a tenth the mass of the earth) and low gravity, such an aqueous atmosphere was assumed ultimately to have escaped, leaving the planet in its present arid state. This view of an earthlike Mars strongly influenced proposals for the biological exploration of the planet at the beginning of the space age. It seemed reasonable to suppose that life could have originated on Mars much as it had on the earth, presumably as the result of high concentrations of suitable precursor molecules in primitive oceans. Once life had appeared on Mars, microorganisms, at least, could very well have been able to adapt to changing environmental conditions and so could have survived for discovery and analysis by robot devices launched from the earth.

Such expectations were dampened by the findings of Mariner 4. Not only did Mars appear bleak and moonlike but also it was found to lack a magnetic field, which could have shielded its surface against energetic charged particles from the sun. Moreover, Mars's atmospheric pressure was found to be less than 1 percent of the earth's, lower by a factor of at least 10 than had previously been estimated. Since the force of gravity at the surface of Mars is more than a third the force of gravity at the surface of the earth, Mars should have easily been able to hold an atmosphere whose pressure at the surface was a tenth the pressure of the earth's atmosphere at the surface.

Mariner 6 and Mariner 7 extended these observations. They confirmed that the polar caps are composed of very pure solid carbon dioxide-"dry ice" rather than water ice. The pictures revealing a chaotic terrain suggested that parts of Mars's surface had collapsed and that there had been a certain amount of internal activity. As a result some investigators speculated that the planet might just now be heating up, a circumstance suggested independently by thermal models of the interior. The preponderant view of the Mariner experimenters, however, was still that Mars was basically more like the moon than like the earth. By then the light and dark markings on Mars seen through telescopes were generally attributed to some kind of atmospheric interaction with dust. Indications that the interaction was controlled by local topography were seen in the second set of Mariner photographs, but no general explanation was deduced. Even so some investigators held to the belief that the markings might instead reflect variations in soil moisture.

The 1971 mission to Mars was originally designed to employ two spacecraft, Mariner 8 and Mariner 9, both of which were to be placed in orbit around the planet. The purpose of the two orbiters was to map most, if not all, of the planet's surface at a resolution high enough to reveal both external and internal processes, to study transient phenomena on the surface and in the atmosphere and to provide reconnaissance over a long enough period (from nine months to a year) to observe seasonal changes in surface markings in the hope of clarifying their origins. When Mariner 8 was lost during launching, the complementary missions of the two spacecraft had to be combined.

When Mariner 9 reached Mars on November 13, 1971, the greatest dust storm in more than a century was raging on the planet, almost totally obscuring its surface. The first views from a distance of several hundred thousand miles revealed essentially no detail except a glimpse of the south polar cap. The dust storm delighted the investigators who wanted to study the planet's atmosphere, since it promised to reveal how particles were transported by such a thin medium, but it was a disappointment to the investigators concerned with surface features. For example, there had been plans to take a sequence of far-encounter pictures, ultimately to be printed in color, showing the planet getting larger and larger, thereby providing a visual bridge between the level of detail seen through telescopes from the earth and the detail eventually visible in pictures taken from orbit around Mars. A limited effort to produce far-encounter pictures showing Mars in natural color had been made with images taken by Mariner 7 through separate red, green and blue filters.

# The Great Volcanoes

The dust storm delayed the systematic mapping of the Martian surface for nearly three months. Even during the storm, however, four dark spots in the equatorial area were repeatedly seen in the early pictures taken from orbit. The spots clearly represented permanent surface features high enough to stick up through the dust. Presumably they looked dark simply because their surface reflectivity was lower than that of the bright, dusty atmosphere.

One of the four spots corresponded to the location of Nix Olympica ("Snows of Olympus"), so named because it was normally visible from the earth as a bright feature and also a variable one. When this dark spot was observed with the high-resolution, or narrow-angle, camera on Mariner 9, the image that emerged was breathtaking. What one saw was the characteristic pattern of coalesced craters that constitute a volcanic caldera. Such calderas are not uncommon on the earth, for example in the Hawaiian Islands. The Martian caldera, however, was 30 times larger in diameter than any in the Hawaiian chain. When the dust had settled, Nix Olympica was seen in full to be an enormous volcanic mountain more than 500 kilometers in diameter at the base, much larger than any similar feature on the earth; the caldera was only the summit. Atmospheric-pressure maps made later with the aid of the ultraviolet spectrometer and other techniques show that Nix Olympica is at least 15 kilometers high and possibly 30. For purposes of comparison, Mauna Loa, the tallest volcanic cone in the Hawaiian Islands, rises less than 10 kilometers from the floor of the Pacific. High-resolution photography revealed that the other three dark spots were also volcanoes, somewhat smaller than Nix Olympica, strung together to form a long volcanic ridge. Following the traditional name for that area, it is now called Tharsis Ridge.

The first recognizable features photographed by Mariner 9 presented a fascinating question: How can one explain why one entire hemisphere of the planet, the hemisphere observed by three earlier Mariners, shows scarcely any evidence of internal activity, whereas the first area to be investigated in detail on the opposite side of the planet has four enormous volcanoes? The explanation apparently is that Mars is just beginning to "boil" inside and produce surface igneous activity. Presumably this process is now well advanced in the Nix Olympica–Tharsis Ridge area but has not yet spread to the planet as a whole. We may be witnessing on Mars a phase similar to one the earth probably went through early in its history, a phase whose record has been totally erased by subsequent igneous and sedimentary processes.

The rate at which a planet's interior heats up depends on a number of factors, chiefly the amount of radioactive material in its original accreted mass and the total mass, which determines the pressure in the interior and the degree of insulation. In very general terms, if Mars had the same original composition as the earth, one would expect it to heat up more slowly because it has only a tenth the mass of the earth. The sheer size of Nix Olympica suggests the possibility that deep convection currents are churning, a process that conceivably could lead some hundreds of millions of years hence to the kind of plate-tectonic phenomena responsible for the slow drift of continents on the earth.

Immediately to the east of the volcanic province is a highly fractured area, and beyond that another extraordinary topographical feature was discovered: a series of huge canyons stretching east and west along the equator. These canyons, 80 to 120 kilometers wide and five to six and a half kilometers deep, are much larger than any found on the earth. Again we must assume that their origin is due to fairly recent internal activity. Presumably large-scale east-west faulting has exposed underlying layers of the planet whose composition could conceivably trigger an erosion process of some kind.

One speculation is that deep permafrost is involved, associated perhaps with the arrival near the surface of juvenile water preceding and accompanying the rise of molten rock near the surface of the planet during the volcanic episode apparent to the west. Mars is everywhere below freezing just a short distance below the surface.

Once permafrost was exposed to the atmosphere, its water content would sublimate, making available a loose, friable material sufficiently mobile to serve as an eroding agent in a mass-transport process. We must then ask where the material went. One possibility is that the winds of Mars have transported it as dust to other localities. (Although the Martian atmosphere is thin, its winds may blow at several hundred miles per hour.) Alternatively, the missing material may yet be discovered somewhere to the east of the canyons. Still a third possibility is that it may even have disappeared into the planet's interior in a complex exchange process.

The largest of the canyons corresponds to a feature long known as Coprates, whose appearance sometimes changes with the seasons. By observing this canyon as the dust storm ended we were able to gain insight into its variable appearance. The canyon is so deep that considerable dust persists in the atmosphere between the canyon walls after the atmosphere above the surrounding region is comparatively dust-free. The dust-filled atmosphere makes the canyon look brighter than the surrounding landscape. Once the canyon atmosphere clears up, there is little contrast between the interior of the canyon and the surrounding area. Hence the variable "surface" markings associated with Coprates probably have nothing to do with the surface at all.

Similar atmospheric processes may well explain some of the other variable markings formerly attributed to seasonal changes. on the surface. Other kinds of variation are not so simply explained, but evidently they always involve the interaction of dust, topography and atmosphere.

Like the volcanoes, the great canyons of Mars suggest a fairly recent episode in the history of the planet characterized by large-scale events. On the earth one often finds a reasonably steady state between processes of erosion and processes of restoration; thus one sees a range of surface morphologies from youthful to mature. In the case of the Martian canyons erosion does not seem to be balanced by a corresponding restoration; we do not see old degraded canyons with a mature form.

# The Channels

The eastern extremity of the canyons joins a large area of chaotic terrain, a small portion of which was glimpsed by Mariner 6. The appearance of the chaotic terrain strongly suggests that it is the result of some kind of collapse and that the collapse is genetically related to the canyons to the west. Extending out from the chaotic terrain in a northwesterly direction are some extraordinary channels, which are also found in a number of other localities on the planet. It is hard to look at these channels without considering the possibility that they were cut by flowing water. Indeed, some of my colleagues think that is the only reasonable explanation.

One can estimate the age of the channels by noting the size-to-frequency relation of impact craters on their floors. The channels are clearly younger than the crater-pocked terrain seen over much of the planet, yet they are by no means the youngest features of the Martian landscape.

The discovery of the channels has revived speculation that there may have been an earthlike epoch in the history of Mars. According to this view Mars may once have had a much denser atmosphere and water vapor in such abundance that rain could fall. Given rainfall, the channels could be easily explained. Less easily explained is why channels have survived in only a few areas and why older topography shows no evidence of water erosion. It would seem difficult to explain how the primitive Martian atmosphere, probably dry and reducing (in the chemical sense), could have evolved into a dense, wet one and then have been transformed again into the present thin, dry atmosphere consisting almost entirely of carbon dioxide. Moreover, the present atmosphere is strongly stabilized by the large amounts of solid carbon dioxide in the polar regions. If the channels were created by rainfall, it would seem that one must postulate two miracles in series: one to create the earthlike atmosphere for a relatively brief epoch and another to destroy it.

An alternative hypothesis presents at least as many difficulties. It is suggested that liquid water accumulated in underground reservoirs following entrapment and melting of permafrost. Hypothetically the reservoirs were abruptly breached, allowing the released water to create the channels. The observed channels are so large and deep, however, that a great volume of water must have been involved in their formation. Therefore it would seem even more difficult to ascribe the channels to a "one shot" open-cycle process than to a closed-cycle process such as rainfall.

The origin of the canyons and channels is one of the primary enigmas that has emerged from the Mariner 9 mission. Because of the importance of liquid water to life as we know it, the possible role of water in creating the canyons and channels has attracted particular interest.

Finally, there are a few areas on Mars to which the term "basins" seems appropriate. The most prominent is the large circular feature Hellas, more than 1,600 kilometers in diameter. Hellas has been observed from the earth for more than two centuries. Sometimes it rivals the polar caps in brightness. Mariner 7 demonstrated that Hellas is indeed a low-lying basin virtually devoid of features. It has been deduced from closeup photographs that the surface of Hellas has probably been smoothed by the influx of large amounts of dust carried into the basin by wind. Mariner 9, however, revealed that Hellas exhibited a few faint topographical features just as the planet-wide dust storm was ending. This suggests that variations in the brightness of Hellas may be due to frequent dust storms of a more local nature, a view originally adduced on meteorological grounds by Carl Sagan of Cornell University and his co-workers. Thus Hellas probably acts as a long-term collection basin for dust but may also serve as a source of dust when the Martian winds blow particularly hard. The observation by Mariner 9 of small-scale dust storms and the recognition that they can alter the brightness of local areas give us further insight into some of the variable features that have been observed over the years from the earth.

One of the crowning achievements of Mariner 7 was the study at high resolutions of the very large polar cap present during the southern winter of 1969. Measurements of reflectivity and temperature provided by an infrared spectrometer and an infrared radiometer on the spacecraft proved conclusively that the south polar cap was composed of very pure solid carbon dioxide, as had been predicted some years earlier. The photographs showed that the frost cover was thin (probably less than a few meters on the average) and that a variety of unusual surface features were also present in the vicinity of the south pole.

When Mariner 9 reached Mars, it was late spring in the southern hemisphere, an ideal time for monitoring the wasting of the dry-ice cap and for examining in detail the unusual surface features that should have been further revealed. The disappearance of the south polar cap started out as expected but then clearly showed anomalous behavior. Curiously, the general outline of the shrunken cap persisted throughout the late summer, when the sublimation of the carbon dioxide should have been at a maximum. This suggested to me that after the large annual cap of carbon dioxide has sublimated, it exposes a residual cap of ordinary water ice. Ordinary ice, of course, has a much lower evaporation rate than carbon dioxide, and traces of water vapor are present in the Martian atmosphere.

Mariner 9's pictures also disclosed a most peculiar terrain in the south polar area, which we named laminated terrain. Although its outline is not symmetrical, it covers much of the south polar region up to about 70 degrees south latitude. The laminated terrain is composed of very thin layers, alternately light and dark, whose gently sloping faces exhibit a certain amount of texture, or relief.

The thin laminas appear to be collected in units of 20 or 30 or more to constitute plates perhaps half a kilometer or more in thickness and up to 200 kilometers across. The plates have outward-facing slopes in which a banded structure can be seen. The laminar deposits have been found only in the polar regions, where carbon dioxide forms an annual deposit of frost. This suggests that the laminations are associated in some way with the coming and going of volatile substances and that they may even retain some solid carbon dioxide or water ice. Since the laminations are marked by very few impact craters, one can deduce that they are a recent development in the history of Mars.

## The North Pole

The north polar region of Mars finally became available for observation by Mariner 9 rather late in the mission as a result of gradual changes in lighting, associated with the change in season and with the lifting of the haze that characteristically develops in the fall over each pole. The quasi circular structures characteristic of laminated terrain were found to be even more abundant around the north pole than around the south pole. One can see 20 or 30 individual plates arranged in a pattern reminiscent of fallen stacks of poker chips. The existence of the laminated terrain and circular-plate structures in the north polar regions as well as in the south polar ones indicates beyond any reasonable doubt that their formation must be associated in some way with the periodic deposition and evaporation of volatile material.

Michael C. Malin, a graduate student at the California Institute of Technology, and I have speculated that the distribution of the circular plates and their overlapping arrangement can be explained by changes in the tilt of Mars's axis. We posit that the rotational axis of the planet has been displaced over the past tens of millions of years as a result of convection currents deep in the mantle, currents that are probably associated with the production of volcanoes in the equatorial areas. As the spin axis has shifted, the laminated plates have formed concentrically around each successive position of the poles.

This speculation is at least consistent with information about Mars's gravity distribution deduced from changes in Mariner 9's orbit. The planet exhibits gravitational anomalies suggestive of deep density differences of the kind that could be associated with deep convection. Moreover, there is a strong correlation between the gravitational anomalies and the location of the equatorial volcanoes.

The regular appearance of the laminas and of the plates themselves suggests that they are also associated in some way with periodic alternations of the climate of Mars. In collaboration with two other graduate students, William Ward and Sze Yeung, I have investigated the theoretical variations in the orbit of Mars over a period of time. We find that perturbations in the orbit caused by other planets, analyzed a number of years ago by Dirk Brouwer and C. M. Clemence, alter the orbit's eccentricity in a way that turns out to be quite favorable for our hypothesis. The eccentricity of Mars's orbit varies from .004, or nearly circular, to .141. Its present value is .09.

The consequence of this variation in eccentricity is a variation in the yearly average amount of sunlight reaching the poles of the planet, together with a much stronger variation in the maximum solar flux when the planet is closest to the sun. Although the variation in average radiant input at the poles is only a few percent, it is sufficient under some circumstances to cause a cyclical variation in the growth and sublimation of permanent carbon dioxide frost caps. Assuming that dust storms regularly deposit dust during the sublimation phases, thin laminas of the type observed could be produced. The plates themselves would therefore correspond to a periodicity of the order of two million years. Hence the laminated terrain seems to closely reflect the fluctuations in average radiant flux reaching the planet both in the short run (roughly 90,000 years) and in the long run (two million years). Inasmuch as a total of 20 or 30 plates are visible in the northern hemisphere the laminated terrain constitutes a record reaching back something like 100 million years. An alternative view regards the origin of the laminated terrain as being primarily erosional rather than constructional.

## Evolution of the Atmosphere

If all the polar laminations accumulated in only a few hundred million years at most, representing no more than the past 5 percent of the history of Mars, what happened earlier? One encounters a basic difficulty in understanding Mars if one tries to apply the famous dictum of the 18th-century geologist James Hutton: "The present is the key to the past." Whether one looks at the volcanic terrain, the canyon lands, the channels or the polar laminations, all seem to record a remarkable degree of activity and change during the most recent part of Mars's geological past. I was led by these considerations to wonder if it is possible that the atmosphere of Mars as we know it may be a fairly recent acquisition. Malin and I are presenting this view as a "contentious speculation." It may be that Mars had no atmosphere at all, or only a very thin, unimportant atmosphere throughout the middle period of its history, lasting perhaps several billion years. Presumably there was an initial primitive atmosphere associated with the accretion of the planet, but this atmosphere may have been lost quite early, particularly if it consisted chiefly of hydrogen and methane.

We think a significant fraction of the mass of the present Martian atmosphere was released during the formation of Nix Olympica and the other three volcanoes in the Tharsis Ridge area. The existence of widespread blankets of rock material and other evidence of somewhat earlier and more extensive volcanism and sedimentation suggest that rather large volumes of volatile substances have issued from the planet's interior in the later geological episodes. Thus it may be that as Mars matured enough to boil it simultaneously began to produce an enduring atmosphere. The atmosphere in turn has produced the laminated terrain and provided the wind-transport and erosion mechanisms to form the channels and the great canyons. On this hypothesis Mars is still far from reaching a steady state in which erosion would be balanced by modification, with a resulting development of a spectrum of morphological features. As part of our contentious speculation one might even imagine that in the early stages of the development of the present Martian atmosphere, before the polar cold traps for carbon dioxide were well established, enough water might have been brought to the surface to have flowed down the channels under peculiar, nonrecurring conditions. At least this possibility avoids the problem of positing two miracles in series and lets us settle for just one if ultimately liquid water is really required to explain the genesis of the channels.

The young-atmosphere hypothesis may also help to explain why "permanent dark areas" (for example the two-pronged feature Sinus Meridiani) should survive in the face of the frequent planet-wide dust storms. Again Mars somehow does not seem to us to be in a steady state, although others do not share our viewpoint. According to our hypothesis the dark markings may be the site of older surface materials not yet affected by the chemical weathering associated with the new atmosphere. In fact, there seems to be some correlation between the permanent dark markings and the terrain populated by the oldest craters.

Other Mariner 9 investigators, such as Sagan and W. K. Hartmann, have developed a quite different view of Mars's history. The nature of the old cratered terrains suggests to them that a long period of atmospheric erosion preceded the spectacular events of the more recent past. Thus the concept of an earthlike Mars is not by any means dead. Nonetheless, concepts of the geological history of Mars are changing rapidly in the light of Mariner 9's highly successful mission. Perhaps ultimately some intermediate interpretation will fit the observations best.

## Is There Life on Mars?

The present Mariner 9 results suggest to me, however, a view very different from that of the early astronomers who thought that Mars was once earthlike and is now a dried-up fossil. I would argue that Mars is probably just now starting to become earthlike with the development of a durable atmosphere. "Just now" is hard to pin down quantitatively because the dates assigned to the craters on the basis of meteor flux rates are still highly uncertain. My guess now would be that the atmospheric "event," if it really happened, took place within the past quarter of Mars's history and certainly within the past half. If this contentious speculation should become widely accepted, it would necessarily imply pessimism about the possibility that past conditions were favorable for the appearance of simple forms of life on Mars. If Mars indeed was like the moon and lacked a significant atmosphere for much of its history, and if the maximum amount of water on the surface has been at most enough to create a few channels, it seems highly unlikely that there has ever been a sufficient accumulation of liquid water in the surface layers of Mars to allow the accidental development of life from prebiological organic materials. On the other hand, life-on-Mars enthusiasts argue otherwise and emphasize that if water has been available at all in surface layers, it would provide a favorable environment for the development of life. Obviously such a debate cannot be settled by the kinds of information collected by Mariner 9. The answer must wait for sophisticated chemical and mineralogical analysis of the surface soil itself.

Simultaneous with the flight of Mariner 9 the U.S.S.R. undertook an ambitious mission whose objective was to land a capsule on Mars and conduct some analyses of the surface. Unfortunately the Russian lander Mars 3 failed shortly after reaching the surface and apparently transmitted no useful information. I expect the U.S.S.R. to repeat this kind of mission late in 1973, and I look forward to seeing pictures from the surface and probably the results of some simple chemical analyses.

One hopes that by 1976 we shall be getting information back from a complex U.S. lander being developed in the Viking program and possibly from a second-generation Russian lander. The Viking capsule is being designed not only to look for organic compounds directly but also to perform some simple but important determinations of the basic inorganic composition of surface minerals. Such measurements will provide an important clue to the past chemical evolution of the surface minerals, including whether or not they have reacted chemically with water.

Will the Viking lander finally tell us if life now exists or ever did exist on Mars? I personally rather doubt it. I think the difficulty of obtaining an unambiguous yes or no is so great that it is probably beyond the grasp of even an investigation as ambitious as the Viking mission. My own view is that the final answer to the great search for life on Mars may have to await the return, probably by unmanned means, of a sample of Martian soil for sophisticated analysis in terrestrial laboratories. My guess is that the U.S.S.R., having demonstrated the ability to return unmanned samples from the moon, should be in a position to repeat this feat for Mars around 1980 (assuming that it continues to give unmanned space exploration the same priority that it has had in the past). The U.S. has no ambitious plans for exploring Mars beyond Viking. Thus Mariner 9 will long be remembered as one of the high points in the American exploration of Mars.

# The Great Martian Storm of '71

By Caleb A. Scharf

O n November 14th 1971 NASA's Mariner 9 became the first spacecraft to successfully orbit another planet. Its video-camera imaging system powered up, and American scientists eagerly awaited the first detailed pictures of Mars since the flyby of Mariners 6 and 7 just two years earlier.

Except what came back from the deep space telemetry were not pictures of the intricate canyons, craters, and mountains of Mars, but pictures of a blanketed world, a dust enshrouded mystery. Mariner 9 had arrived in the midst of one of the greatest global storms humans have ever witnessed on Mars.

It wasn't a total surprise for the scientists, earlier observations had hinted at a dust storm that began in late September of that year in the southern Noachis Terra landmass. But the extent of this system was astonishing. There was essentially nothing visible of the martian surface.

In another first for interplanetary exploration, the NASA engineers reprogrammed the spacecraft to wait the storm out. This was quite a feat, the computer was extraordinarily primitive by today's standards, as was the data storage. Here's a quote from the NASA NSSDC page detailing Mariner 9's specs:

> "Spacecraft control was through the central computer and sequencer which had an onboard memory of 512 words. The command system was programmed with 86 direct commands, 4 quantitative commands, and 5 control commands. Data was stored on a digital reel-to-reel tape recorder. The 168 meter 8-track tape could store 180 million bits recorded at 132 kbits/s. Playback could be done at 16, 8, 4, 2, and 1 kbit/s using two tracks at a time."

In the meantime the Soviet mission Mars 2 arrived just two weeks after Mariner 9, but it didn't have the option to reprogram, and automatically sent its lander probe down to the surface and right into the dust. It's not clear exactly what went wrong, but barreling out of space and into a thick storm of micron-sized dust particles probably didn't help the probe's chances, and it summarily crashed on the surface.

By late 1971 and into January 1972 the storm abated, and Mariner 9 began to send back some spectacular images—a total of over 7,300 pictures that mapped the entire martian surface with resolutions ranging from 1 kilometer per pixel to as good at 100 meters per pixel.

The images give a sense of the magnitude of the storm, as well as was what the scientists began to see as the dust settled. The only visible features were the three great Tharsis Montes shield volcanoes, poking up through the haze in a line. The tallest of these reaches an altitude of over 18 kilometers. These peaks, and the enormous bulk of Olympus Mons had never been imaged by a spacecraft before, earlier flybys had missed them.

The late Bruce Murray (Caltech) was on the camera team and recalls, "there was a gradual clearing, like a stage scene, and three dark spots showed up." The Mars that came out of the storm was a revelation, from these colossal mountains to the great rift of Valles Marineris and the steep valleys of Noctis Labyrinthus.

It was good that the storm cleared when it did. These images and the global map from Mariner 9 paved the way for the extremely successful Viking missions, and helped pinpoint where the landers should try to set down.

Since then we've seen plenty of other dust storms on Mars. In fact, in 2001 NASA's Mars Global Surveyor was witness to another planet-scale event—possibly comparable in size to the 1971 storm.

You can see a time sequence of Global Surveyor full-globe images at Malin Space Science Systems, spanning June 2001 to September 2001. The whole planet was engulfed—a scene also captured by the Hubble Space Telescope.

With data from Global Surveyor we learned that although the dust reflects much of the sunlight hitting Mars during the day, thereby cooling the surface, the particles also absorb radiation and re-emit it as infrared (heat) at night. The upshot is that while the surface chills under its dusty blanket, the atmosphere actually heats up, by as much as 30 Celsius. This may be a clue to how such storms go global—a warmer atmosphere can drive stronger winds that lift more dust off the surface.

While Mariner 9's first view of the red planet may have been a disappointment, it was also a glimpse into the remarkable environment on another world. It's an environment that continues to fascinate, as well as provide a calibration point for our understanding of small rocky planets that are unlike the Earth.

Indeed, the thermal signature of planet-wide dust storms might be something we could keep an eye out for when the first direct glimpses of terrestrial-scale exoplanets are obtained. Even if we can't see these worlds as anything more than a point of light, their varying spectral character could be familiar, a sight we'd recognize from that stormy day on Mars in 1971.

*The views expressed are those of the author(s) and are not necessarily those of Scientific American.*

## About the Author

*Caleb A. Scharf is director of astrobiology at Columbia University. He is author and co-author of more than 100 scientific research articles in astronomy and astrophysics. His work has been featured in publications such as* New Scientist, Scientific American, Science News, Cosmos Magazine, Physics Today *and* National Geographic. *For many years he wrote the* Life, Unbounded *blog for* Scientific American.

# The Mars Pathfinder Mission

By Matthew P. Golombek

R ocks, rocks, look at those rocks," I exclaimed to everyone in the Mars Pathfinder control room at about 4:30 P.M. on July 4, 1997. The Pathfinder lander was sending back its first images of the surface of Mars, and everyone was focused on the television screens. We had gone to Mars to look at rocks, but no one knew for sure whether we would find any, because the landing site had been selected using orbital images with a resolution of roughly a kilometer. Pathfinder could have landed on a flat, rock-free plain. The first radio downlink indicated that the lander was nearly horizontal, which was worrisome for those of us interested in rocks, as most expected that a rocky surface would result in a tilted lander. The very first images were of the lander so that we could ascertain its condition, and it was not until a few tense minutes later that the first pictures of the surface showed a rocky plain—exactly as we had hoped and planned for.

Why did we want rocks? Every rock carries the history of its formation locked in its minerals, so we hoped the rocks would tell us about the early Martian environment. The two-part Pathfinder payload, consisting of a main lander with a multispectral camera and a mobile rover with a chemical analyzer, was suited to looking at rocks. Although it could not identify the minerals directly—its analyzer could measure only their constituent chemical elements—our plan was to identify them indirectly based on the elemental composition and the shapes, textures and colors of the rocks. By landing Pathfinder at the mouth of a giant channel where a huge volume of water once flowed briefly, we sought rocks that had washed down from the ancient, heavily cratered highlands. Such rocks could offer clues to the early climate of Mars and to whether conditions were once conducive to the development of life.

The most important requirement for life on Earth (the only kind we know) is liquid water. Under present conditions on Mars, liquid water is unstable: because the temperature and pressure are so low, water is stable only as ice or vapor; liquid would survive for just a brief time before freezing or evaporating. Yet Viking images taken two decades ago show drainage channels and evidence for lakes in the highlands. These features hint at a warmer and wetter past on Mars in which water could persist on the surface. To be sure, other explanations have also been suggested, such as sapping processes driven by geothermal heating in an otherwise frigid and dry environment. One of Pathfinder's scientific goals was to look for evidence of a formerly warm, wet Mars.

The possible lakebeds are found in terrain that, judging from its density of impact craters, is roughly the same age as the oldest rocks on Earth, which show clear evidence for life 3.9 billion to 3.6 billion years ago. If life was able to develop on Earth at this time, why not on Mars, too, if the conditions were similar? This is what makes studying Mars so compelling. By exploring our neighboring planet, we can seek answers to some of the most important questions in science: Are we alone in the universe? Will life arise anywhere that liquid water is stable, or does the formation of life require something else as well? And if life did develop on Mars, what happened to it? If life did not develop, why not?

## Pathfinding

Pathfinder was a Discovery-class mission—one of the National Aeronautics and Space Administration's "faster, cheaper, better" spacecraft—to demonstrate a low-cost means of landing a small payload and mobile vehicle on Mars. It was developed, launched and operated under a fixed budget comparable to that of a major motion picture (between $200 million and $300 million), which is a mere fraction of the budget typically allocated for space missions. Built and launched in a short time (three and a half years), Pathfinder included three science instruments: the Imager for Mars Pathfinder, the Alpha Proton X-Ray Spectrometer and the Atmospheric Structure Instrument/Meteorology Package. The rover itself also acted as an instrument; it was used to conduct 10 technology experiments, which studied the abrasion of metal films on a rover wheel and the adherence of dust to a solar cell as well as other ways the equipment reacted to its surroundings.

In comparison, the Viking mission, which included two orbiter-lander pairs, was carried out more than 20 years ago at roughly 20 times the cost. Viking was very successful, returning more than 57,000 images that scientists have been studying ever since. The landers carried sophisticated experiments that tested for organisms at two locations; they found none.

The hardest part of Pathfinder's mission was the five minutes during which the spacecraft went from the relative security of interplanetary cruising to the stress of atmospheric entry, descent and landing. In that short time, more than 50 critical events had to be triggered at exactly the right times for the spacecraft to land safely. About 30 minutes before entry, the backpack-style cruise stage separated from the rest of the lander. At 130 kilometers above the surface, the spacecraft entered the atmosphere behind a protective aeroshell. A parachute unfurled 134 seconds before landing, and then the aeroshell was jettisoned. During descent, the lander was lowered beneath its back cover on a 20-meter-long bridle, or tether.

As Pathfinder approached the surface, its radar altimeter triggered the firing of three small rockets to slow it down further. Giant air bags inflated around each face of the tetrahedral lander, the bridle was cut and the lander bounced onto the Martian surface at 50 kilometers per hour. Accelerometer measurements indicate that the air-bag-enshrouded lander bounced at least 15 times without losing air-bag pressure. After rolling at last to a stop, the lander deflated the air bags and opened to begin surface operations.

Although demonstrating this novel landing sequence was actually Pathfinder's primary goal, the rest of the mission also met or exceeded expectations. The lander lasted three times longer than its minimum design criteria, the rover 12 times longer. The mission returned 2.3 billion bits of new data from Mars, including more than 16,500 lander and 550 rover images and roughly 8.5 million individual temperature, pressure and wind measurements. The rover traversed a total of 100 meters in 230 commanded movements, thereby exploring more than 200 square meters of the surface. It obtained 16 measurements of rock and soil chemistry, performed soil-mechanics experiments and successfully completed the numerous technology experiments. The mission also captured the imagination of the public, garnering front-page headlines for a week, and became the largest Internet event in history, with a total of about 566 million hits for the first month of the mission—47 million on July 8 alone.

## Flood Stage

The mosaic of the landscape constructed from the first images revealed a rocky plain (about 20 percent of which was covered by rocks) that appears to have been deposited and shaped by catastrophic floods. This was what we had predicted based on remote-sensing data and the location of the landing site (19.13 degrees north, 33.22 degrees west), which is downstream from the mouth of Ares Vallis in the low area known as Chryse Planitia. In Viking orbiter images, the area appears analogous to the Channeled Scabland in eastern and central Washington State. This analogy suggests that Ares Vallis formed when roughly the same volume of water as in the Great Lakes (hundreds of cubic kilometers) was catastrophically released, carving the observed channel in a few weeks. The density of impact craters in the region indicates it formed at an intermediate time in Mars's history, somewhere between 1.8 billion and 3.5 billion years ago.

The Pathfinder images support this interpretation. They show semirounded pebbles, cobbles and boulders similar to those deposited by terrestrial catastrophic floods. Rocks in what we dubbed the Rock Garden, a collection of rocks to the southwest of the lander, with the names Shark, Half Dome and Moe, are inclined and stacked, as if deposited by rapidly flowing water. Large rocks in the images (0.5 meter or larger) are flat-topped and often perched, also consistent with deposition by a flood. Twin Peaks, a pair of hills on the southwest horizon, are streamlined. Viking images suggest that the lander is on the flank of a broad, gentle ridge trending northeast from Twin Peaks; this ridge may be a debris tail deposited in the wake of the peaks. Small channels throughout the scene resemble those in the Channeled Scabland, where drainage in the last stage of the flood preferentially removed fine-grained materials.

The rocks in the scene are dark gray and covered with various amounts of yellowish-brown dust. This dust appears to be the same as that seen in the atmosphere, which, as imaging in different filters and locations in the sky suggests, is very fine grained (a micron in size). The dust also collected in wind streaks behind rocks.

Some of the rocks have been fluted and grooved, presumably by sand-size particles (less than one millimeter) that hopped along the surface in the wind. The rover's camera also saw sand dunes in the trough behind the Rock Garden. Dirt covers the lower few centimeters of some rocks, suggesting that they have been exhumed by wind. Despite these signs of slow erosion by the wind, the rocks and surface appear to have changed little since they were deposited by the flood.

## Sedimentary Rocks on Mars?

The Alpha Proton X-Ray Spectrometer on the rover measured the compositions of eight rocks. The silicon content of some of the rocks is much higher than that of the Martian meteorites, our only other samples of Mars. The Martian meteorites are all mafic igneous rocks, volcanic rocks that are relatively low in silicon and high in iron and magnesium. Such rocks form when the upper mantle of a planet melts. The melt rises up through the crust and solidifies at or near the surface. These types of rocks, referred to as basalts, are the most common rock on Earth and have also been found on the moon. Based on the composition of the Martian meteorites and the presence of plains and mountains that look like features produced by basaltic volcanism on Earth, geologists expected to find basalts on Mars.

The rocks analyzed by Pathfinder, however, are not basalts. If they are volcanic, as suggested by their vesicular surface texture, presumably formed when gases trapped during cooling left small holes in the rock, their silicon content classifies them as andesites.

Andesites form when the basaltic melt from the mantle intrudes deep within the crust. Crystals rich in iron and magnesium form and sink back down, leaving a more silicon-rich melt that erupts onto the surface. The andesites were a great surprise, but because we do not know where these rocks came from on the Martian surface, we do not know the full implications of this discovery. If the andesites are representative of the highlands, they suggest that ancient crust on Mars is similar in composition to continental crust on Earth. This similarity would be difficult to reconcile with the very different geologic histories of the two planets. Alternatively, the rocks could represent a minor proportion of high-silicon rocks from a predominately basaltic plain.

Intriguingly, not all the rocks appear to be volcanic. Some have layers like those in terrestrial sedimentary rocks, which form by deposition of smaller fragments of rocks in water. Indeed, rover images show many rounded pebbles and cobbles on the ground. In addition, some larger rocks have what look like embedded pebbles and shiny indentations, where it looks as though rounded pebbles that were pressed into the rock during its formation have fallen out, leaving holes. These rocks may be conglomerates formed by flowing liquid water. The water would have rounded the pebbles and deposited them in a sand, silt and clay matrix; the matrix was subsequently compressed, forming a rock, and carried to its present location by the flood. Because conglomerates require a long time to form, if these Martian rocks are conglomerates they strongly suggest that liquid water was once stable and that the climate was therefore warmer and wetter than at present.

Soils at the landing site vary from the bright-red dust to darker-red and darker-gray material. Overall, the soils are lower in silicon than the rocks and richer in sulfur, iron and magnesium. Soil compositions are generally the same as those measured at the Viking sites, which are on opposite hemispheres (Viking 1 is 800 kilometers west of Pathfinder; Viking 2 is thousands of kilometers away on the opposite, eastern side of the northern hemisphere). Thus, this soil may be a globally deposited unit.

35

The similarity in compositions among the soils implies that their differences in color may be the result of slight variations in iron mineralogy or in particle size and shape.

A bright-red or pink material also covered part of the site. Similar to the soils in composition, it seems to be indurated or cemented because it was not damaged by scraping with the rover wheels. Pathfinder also investigated the dust in the atmosphere of Mars by observing its deposition on a series of magnetic targets on the spacecraft. The dust, it turned out, is highly magnetic. It may consist of small silicate (perhaps clay) particles, with some stain or cement of a highly magnetic mineral known as maghemite. This finding, too, is consistent with a watery past. The iron may have dissolved out of crustal materials in water, and the maghemite may be a freeze-dried precipitate.

The sky on Mars had the same butterscotch color as it did when imaged by the Viking landers. Fine-grained dust in the atmosphere would explain this color. Hubble Space Telescope images had suggested a very clear atmosphere; scientists thought it might even appear blue from the surface. But Pathfinder found otherwise, suggesting either that the atmosphere always has some dust in it from local dust storms or that the atmospheric opacity varies appreciably over a short time. The inferred dust-particle size (roughly a micron) and shape and the amount of water vapor (equivalent to a pitiful hundredth of a millimeter of rainfall) in the atmosphere are also consistent with measurements made by Viking. Even if Mars was once lush, it is now drier and dustier than any desert on Earth.

## Freezing Air

The meteorological sensors gave further information about the atmosphere. They found patterns of diurnal and longer-term pressure and temperature fluctuations. The temperature reached its maximum of 263 kelvins (–10 degrees Celsius) every day at 2:00 P.M. local solar time and its minimum of 197 kelvins (–76 degrees C) just before sunrise. The pressure minimum of just under 6.7 millibars (roughly 0.67 percent of pressure at sea level on Earth) was reached on sol 20, the 20th Martian day after landing. On Mars the air pressure varies with the seasons. During winter, it is so cold that 20 to 30 percent of the entire atmosphere freezes out at the pole, forming a huge pile of solid carbon dioxide. The pressure minimum seen by Pathfinder indicates that the atmosphere was at its thinnest, and the south polar cap its largest, on sol 20.

Morning temperatures fluctuated abruptly with time and height; the sensors positioned 0.25, 0.5 and one meter above the spacecraft took different readings. If you were standing on Mars, your nose would be at least 20 degrees C colder than your feet. This suggests that cold morning air is warmed by the surface and rises in small eddies, or whirlpools, which is very different from what happens on Earth, where such large temperature disparities do not occur. Afternoon temperatures, after the air has warmed, do not show these variations.

In the early afternoon, dust devils repeatedly swept across the lander. They showed up as sharp, short-lived pressure changes and were probably similar to events detected by the Viking landers and orbiters; they may be an important mechanism for raising dust into the Martian atmosphere. Otherwise, the prevailing winds were light (clocked at less than 36 kilometers per hour) and variable.

Pathfinder measured atmospheric conditions at higher altitudes during its descent. The upper atmosphere (altitude above 60 kilometers) was colder than Viking had measured. This finding may simply reflect seasonal variations and the time of entry: Pathfinder came in at 3:00 A.M. local solar time, whereas Viking arrived at 4:00 P.M., when the atmosphere is naturally warmer. The lower atmosphere was similar to that measured by Viking, and its conditions can be attributed to dust mixed uniformly in comparatively warm air.

As a bonus, mission scientists were able to use radio communications signals from Pathfinder to measure the rotation of Mars. Daily Doppler tracking and less frequent two-way ranging during communication sessions determined the position of the lander with a precision of 100 meters. The last such positional measurement was done by Viking more than 20 years ago. In the interim, the pole of rotation has precessed—that is, the direction of the tilt of the planet has changed, just as a spinning top slowly wobbles. The difference between the two positional measurements yields the precession rate. The rate is governed by the moment of inertia of the planet, a function of the distribution of mass within the planet. The moment of inertia had been the single most important number about Mars that we did not yet know.

From Pathfinder's determination of the moment of inertia we now know that Mars must have a central metallic core that is between 1,300 and 2,400 kilometers in radius. With assumptions about the mantle composition, derived from the compositions of the Martian meteorites and the rocks measured by the rover, scientists can now start to put constraints on interior temperatures. Before Pathfinder, the composition of the Martian meteorites argued for a core, but the size of this core was completely unknown. The new information about the interior will help geophysicists understand how Mars has evolved over time. In addition to the long-term precession, Pathfinder detected an annual variation in the planet's rotation rate, which is just what would be expected from the seasonal exchange of carbon dioxide between the atmosphere and the ice caps.

Taking all the results together suggests that Mars was once more Earth-like than previously appreciated. Some crustal materials on Mars resemble, in silicon content, continental crust on Earth. Moreover, the rounded pebbles and the possible conglomerate, as well as the abundant sand- and dust-size particles, argue for a formerly water-rich planet. The earlier environment may have been warmer and wetter, perhaps similar to that of the early Earth. In contrast, since floods produced the landing site 1.8 billion to 3.5 billion years ago, Mars has been a very un-Earth-like place. The site appears almost unaltered since it was deposited, indicating very low erosion rates and thus no water in relatively recent times.

Although we are not certain that early Mars was more like Earth, the data returned from Pathfinder are very suggestive. Information from the Mars Global Surveyor, now orbiting the Red Planet, should help answer this crucial question about our neighboring world.

## Referenced

Mars. Edited by Hugh H. Kieffer, Bruce M. Jakosky, Conway W. Snyder and Mildred S. Matthews. University of Arizona Press, 1992.

Water on Mars. Michael H. Carr. Oxford University Press, 1996.

Mars Pathfinder Mission and Ares Vallis Landing Site. Matthew P. Golombek et al. in Journal of Geophysical Research, Vol. 102, No. E2, pages 3951-4229; February 25, 1997.

Mars Pathfinder. Matthew P. Golombek et al. in Science, Vol. 278, pages 1734-1774; December 5, 1997.

## About the Author

Matthew P. Golombek is project scientist of Mars Pathfinder, with responsibility for the overall scientific content of the mission. He conducts his work at the Jet Propulsion Laboratory in Pasadena, Calif. He is chair of the Pathfinder Project Science Group, deputy of the Experiment Operations Team and a member of the project management group. He has written numerous papers on the spacecraft and its results and has organized press conferences and scientific meetings. Golombek's research focuses on the structural geology and tectonics of Earth and the other planets, particularly Mars. He became interested in geology because he wanted to know why Earth had mountains and valleys.

# A New Way to Reach Mars Safely, Anytime and on the Cheap

By Adam Hadhazy

Getting spacecraft to Mars is quite a hassle. Transportation costs can soar into the hundreds of millions of dollars, even when blasting off during "launch windows"–the optimal orbital alignments of Earth and Mars that roll around only every 26 months. A huge contributor to that bottom line? The hair-raising arrivals at the Red Planet. Spacecraft screaming along at many thousands of kilometers per hour have to hit the brakes hard, firing retrorockets to swing into orbit. The burn can require hundreds of pounds of extra fuel, lugged expensively off Earth, and comes with some risk of failure that could send the craft careening past or even right into Mars.

This brute force approach to attaining orbit, called a Hohmann transfer, has served historically deep-pocketed space agencies well enough. But in an era of shrinking science budgets the Hohmann transfer's price tag and inherent riskiness look limiting.

Now new research lays out a smoother, safer way to achieve Martian orbit without being restricted by launch windows or busting the bank. Called ballistic capture, it could help open the Martian frontier for more robotic missions, future manned expeditions and even colonization efforts. "It's an eye-opener," says James Green, director of NASA's Planetary Science Division. "It could be a pretty big step for us and really save us resources and capability, which is always what we're looking for."

The premise of a ballistic capture: Instead of shooting for the location Mars will be in its orbit where the spacecraft will meet it, as is conventionally done with Hohmann transfers, a spacecraft is casually lobbed into a Mars-like orbit so that it flies ahead of the planet. Although launch and cruise costs remain the same, the big burn to slow down and hit the Martian bull's-eye—as in the Hohmann scenario—is done away with. For ballistic capture, the spacecraft cruises a bit slower than Mars itself as the planet runs its orbital lap around the sun. Mars eventually creeps up on the spacecraft, gravitationally snagging it into a planetary orbit. "That's the magic of ballistic capture—it's like flying in formation," says Edward Belbruno, a visiting associated researcher at Princeton University and co-author, with Francesco Topputo of the Polytechnic University of Milan, of a paper detailing the new path to Mars and the physics behind it. The paper, posted on *arXiv*, has been submitted to the journal *Celestial Mechanics and Dynamical Astronomy*.

## "A Delicate Dance"

Ballistic capture, also called a low-energy transfer, is not in of itself a new idea. While at NASA's Jet Propulsion Laboratory a quarter century ago, Belbruno laid out the fuel-saving, cost-shaving orbital insertion method for coasting probes to the Moon. A Japanese vessel, called Hiten, first took advantage in 1991, as did NASA's GRAIL mission, launched in 2011.

Belbruno worked out how to let the competing gravities of Earth, the sun and moon gently pull a spacecraft into a desired lunar orbit. All three bodies can be thought of as creating bowl-like depressions in spacetime. By lining up the trajectory of a spacecraft through those bowls, such that momentum slackens along the route, a spacecraft can just "roll" down at the end into the moon's small bowl, easing into orbit fuel-free. "It's a delicate dance," Belbruno says.

Unfortunately, pulling off a similar maneuver at Mars (or anywhere else) seemed impossible because the Red Planet's velocity is much higher than the Moon's. There appeared no way to get a spacecraft to slow down enough to glide into Mars' gravitational spacetime depression because the "bowl," not that deep to begin with, was itself a too-rapidly moving target. "I gave up on it," Belbruno says.

However, while recently consulting for the Boeing Corp., the major contractor for NASA's Space Launch System, which is intended to take humankind to Mars, Belbruno, Topputo and colleagues stumbled on an idea: Why not go with the flow near Mars? Sailing a spacecraft into an orbital path anywhere from a million to even tens of millions of kilometers ahead of the Red Planet would make it possible for Mars (and its spacetime bowl) to ease into the spacecraft's vicinity, thus subsequently letting the spacecraft be ballistically captured. Boeing, intrigued by this novel avenue to Mars, funded the study, in which the authors crunched some numbers and developed models for the capture.

## Expanding Our Martian Horizons

Ballistic capture is not the only fuel-saving technique for entering orbit. In another approach, called aerocapture, an arriving spacecraft dives into the Martian atmosphere and lets friction eat away at some of its excess velocity, rather than relying solely on a big fuel burn to do the trick. That method, however, requires a heavy heat shield, which adds extra mass and thus costs to liftoff, offsetting the penny-pinching on fuel for a Hohmann transfer burn on arrival. Ballistic capture, Topputo says, is "slower and gentler."

Ballistic capture therefore offers many advantages over current approaches for heading to Mars. Beyond avoiding the fuel-guzzling of a Hohmann transfer, for instance, it reduces danger to the craft because the vessel no longer must decelerate on a dime in a tight window near Mars, risking over- or undershooting its mark. The approach also drops fuel needs for the overall journey by 25 percent, Belbruno says, in a rough estimate. That reduction could be used to save money but it could also, instead, allow for bigger payloads at comparable prices. Delivering more mass to Martian orbit can then mean getting more robotic rovers, supplies or what have you to the surface. "What we want to do is leverage [ballistic capture] to put more mass on the ground," Green says. "That's the dream." Avoiding the need to send the rocket up during rare launch windows would also be a big deal because launch delays are notoriously frequent. Missing a window can mean grounding a Mars mission for two years, plus wasted launch prep costs.

# For 'Bots, as well as Bodies?

Ballistic capture does come with plenty of caveats, of course. A straight shot with abrupt braking at Mars takes about six months whereas a trip relying on ballistic capture would take an additional several months. The burn-free, capture altitude is also quite high—some 20,000 kilometers above Mars, far beyond where science satellites set up shop to scrutinize the planet up close. But taking along just a little extra fuel can then gently lower a ballistically captured spacecraft into scientifically valuable, standard orbits of around 100 to 200 kilometers like those achieved with Hohmann transfers—or even onward to the Martian surface for a landing.

For manned missions, ballistic transfer would be a mixed blessing. On one hand, its longer journeys would add to the challenges of ferrying people to Mars. We're already worried about Mars-bound explorers driving each other crazy stuck in a tin can for six months, not to mention soaking up unacceptably high space radiation doses. For that reason, robotic missions look to be the first potential beneficiaries of Belbruno and Topputo's new low-energy transfers.

On the other hand, because the need for launch windows would go away, ballistic capture could maintain a steady stream of supplies to the planet. Any extended Mars habitation effort would probably depend on Earth for materiel, at least until the establishment of self-sufficient farming and manufacturing. "Ballistic capture would be a good way to send supplies to Mars in advance of a manned mission," Belbruno says, "or as part of one."

NASA's Green agrees. "This [ballistic capture technique] could not only apply here to the robotic end of it but also the human exploration end," he says. Accordingly, Green arranged for Belbruno to speak with the agency's Johnson Space Center staff back in October about how manned missions might exploit the concept.

Even further down the road, ballistic capture would be perfect, Belbruno says, for placing satellites into "areostationary" orbits—the same as geostationary, except at Mars (aka Ares). The upshot: Martian Internet and cell phone networks, anyone? If the new low-energy transfer works at Mars, it could, in theory, also be extended to deliver matter in bulk to any world in the solar system.

This potential breakthrough research is admittedly still in an early, theoretical phase. Ongoing work includes reworking the calculations of the physics by factoring in smaller influences on a Mars-bound spacecraft than the pull of gravity from Mars itself, such as Jupiter's gravitational pull. NASA's Green said he envisions the agency wanting to test ballistic capture transfers at Mars in the 2020s. Belbruno has his fingers crossed. "The route to the moon I found in 1991 was thought to be perhaps the only application of my theory," he says. "I am very excited about this Mars result."

# China Lands Tianwen-1 Rover on Mars in a Major First for the Country

By Jonathan O'Callaghan

And then there were two: today China says it safely landed a spacecraft on Mars—for the first time in its history and in its first attempt—becoming the only other nation besides the U.S. to achieve such a feat. Its Zhurong rover, named after a god of fire from Chinese folklore, successfully touched down in Utopia Planitia around 7:18 P.M. EST as part of the Tianwen-1 mission, according to the China National Space Administration. Soon the rover should drive down the ramp of its landing platform, ready to explore its unearthly surroundings. If there was any doubt about China's spacefaring prowess, it has been dispelled now that the nation has added interplanetary landings as a coveted notch on its belt. "Mars is hard," says Roger Launius, NASA's former chief historian. "This is a really big deal."

Tianwen-1 was launched in July 2020 as part of a summer Martian armada that also included launches of NASA's Perseverance rover and the United Arab Emirates' Hope orbiter. All three missions arrived at Mars in February. But while Perseverance descended straight to the surface, Tianwen-1 instead entered an elliptical orbit around the planet to give its scientists a god's-eye view for scouting out their planned landing site in Utopia Planitia, an immense impact basin on Mars. "China does not have its own detailed Mars maps," says Brian Harvey, a writer who covers the country's space program. At least, that was the case until today, when Tianwen-1's controllers decided they had seen enough to confidently initiate the spacecraft's daring descent.

Packed inside a cone-shaped protective shell, Zhurong and its rocket-powered landing platform detached from the orbiter, descended toward Mars and began the fiery plunge through the planet's upper atmosphere. After jettisoning its protective shell lower in the atmosphere, the spacecraft unfurled parachutes to slow its descent before riding thrusters down to a gentle landing on the surface. This was "very similar" to the powered landings China has used in its Chang'e missions to Earth's moon, says Andrew Jones, a space journalist who follows the Chinese space program. The latest of those missions returned samples to Earth in 2020.

Other nations have tried and failed to land on Mars, but China's success highlights how it is rapidly catching up to, if not exceeding, many of its counterparts. The Soviet Union notably attempted multiple landings in the 1970s, coming closest with Mars 3, which touched down on the planet but stopped working moments later. The U.K. reached the surface with its Beagle 2 lander in 2003. The craft's communications antenna failed to deploy, however, dooming the mission. The European Space Agency (ESA) and Russia also came close with their Schiaparelli lander—until it crashed on Mars in 2016. ESA will try again with its Rosalind Franklin rover in 2022. Until today, only the U.S. had successfully operated any spacecraft on Mars for a significant period of time, starting with the Viking landers of 1976 and extending to the country's multiple landers and rovers that are exploring the surface today. China now joins this most elite and exclusive of clubs. "It's a big day for China," says Mark McCaughrean, senior scientific adviser for science and exploration at ESA. "We know better than anyone how hard it can be to get safely down to the surface."

China will now wait an undisclosed amount of time, as little as a day or up to perhaps a week, before driving the Zhurong rover down a ramp from the lander and onto the surface. The six-wheeled solar-powered vehicle has a planned lifetime of 90 Martian days and is thought to have a top speed of 200 meters per hour, Jones says, although it will likely explore much more slowly. China will upload commands to the rover via its Tianwen-1 orbiter, with ESA's Mars Express orbiter acting as a backup. The rover will then perform its tasks autonomously on the surface, similar to the operational protocols NASA uses for its own fleet of robotic Martian explorers.

Utopia Planitia was also the site for NASA's Viking 2 in 1976. It is a rather bland expanse of rock-strewn sand—decent for spacecraft landings but decidedly subpar for addressing cutting-edge research questions, such as whether Mars harbors past or present life. "[China is] not looking for biosignatures," says Agnes Cousin, a planetary scientist at the Institute for Research in Astrophysics and Planetology in France, who has advised Tianwen-1 scientists. Yet Zhurong is still expected to perform important science on the surface of the Red Planet. "We always have surprises when we arrive on the surface," Cousin says. "For the overall geological implications for Mars, it's very nice to have a new location to compare."

The rover is equipped with a suite of six instruments and cameras to study the surface. They include a ground-penetrating radar that could look for water and ice up to 100 meters below the surface (NASA's Perseverance boasts a similar instrument). Zhurong also has a magnetometer, the first ever sent to Mars on a rover. Alongside a similar instrument on the Tianwen-1 orbiter, which will continue studying the planet from afar, the rover's magnetometer could reveal the details of how Mars lost its magnetic field—and consequently its atmosphere and water—billions of years ago. "Conceivably this instrument could help address that question," says David Flannery, an astrobiologist at the Queensland University of Technology in Australia, who is familiar with China's space activities. "Together the instruments will tell us more about how the Martian magnetic field operates today."

Another instrument of note is the Mars Surface Composition Detector (MarSCoDe), a device similar to ChemCam on NASA's Curiosity rover and SuperCam on Perseverance, which will use a laser to vaporize rock specimens on the surface, revealing their composition. Cousin is part of both the ChemCam and SuperCam teams, and she was among a group of European collaborators that helped China develop their instrument. She traveled to Shanghai in 2019 to exchange information with Tianwen-1 scientists on topics such as data-processing techniques and calibration targets to include on the rover to test the instrument on Mars. "They wanted big calibration targets" for MarSCoDe, Cousin says. "So we gave them one": a two-centimeter-wide square of an igneous rock called norite that is one of 12 such targets on the rover.

While the science goals of the rover may be somewhat modest, it is also expected to be a technology demonstration for a much more ambitious future project. By 2028 or 2030, China hopes to send a sample-return mission to Mars to bring pristine Martian rocks back to Earth. That timing is similar to, or perhaps even in advance of, when NASA and ESA plan to do the same with their own interplanetary grab-and-go effort. "Will it be China bringing the first Mars material back to Earth, or will it be NASA and ESA?" says Jacqueline Myrrhe, a journalist affiliated with the Chinese space Web site Go Taikonauts! "This could be a very good question."

Landing on Mars is the latest pinnacle achievement from China's planned portfolio of ambitious space activities. But already the nation has more than proved its mettle. It has conducted numerous sorties to the moon and has begun the construction of a space station in Earth orbit. The nation may send a pair of spacecraft to the edge of the solar system in just a few years and launch a mission to Jupiter by the end of the decade. Now that Tianwen-1 has shown that China is an adept interplanetary explorer, even more audacious projects may be on the horizon. "It's the first step for much more," Myrrhe says.

## About the Author

*Jonathan O'Callaghan is a freelance journalist covering commercial spaceflight, space exploration and astrophysics. Follow him on Twitter @Astro_Jonny.*

# Section 2: Possible Mars Settlements

2.1    Human Missions to Mars Will Look Completely Different from *The Martian*
     By Lee Billings

2.2    Is "Protecting" Mars from Contamination a Half-Baked Idea?
     By Michael J. Battaglia

2.3    Can Mars Be Terraformed?
     By Christopher Edwards and Bruce Jakosky

2.4    Aerogel Mars
     By Caleb A. Scharf

2.5    Surviving Mars
     By Caleb A. Scharf

2.6    How to Grow Vegetables on Mars
     By Edward Guinan, Scott Engle, and Alicia Eglin

# Human Missions to Mars Will Look Completely Different from *The Martian*

By Lee Billings

L anding in U.S. theaters today, Ridley Scott's *The Martian* is being acclaimed as one of the most realistic portrayals of human space exploration ever filmed. Based on the 2011 novel by Andy Weir, the film stars Matt Damon as Mark Watney, a wisecracking botanist-turned-astronaut marooned on Mars after being accidentally left behind by his crewmates. Faced with extremely limited food and supplies, and with any hope of rescue more than a year and millions of kilometers away, early on Watney lays out his stark options for subsistence in the film's most memorable line of dialogue: Either "science the shit out of this," or die.

Incidentally, it's not really science that Watney uses to survive—it's engineering. But whatever you call it, the result is a wonderfully entertaining and reasonably accurate portrayal of how to live off the land—even when that land is on a freeze-dried alien planet.

As NASA workers struggle to launch a mission to bring him back home, Watney improvises one ingenious scheme after another to stay alive. He turns his habitat into a chemistry lab and a greenhouse, extracting potable water from rocket fuel and growing potatoes in nutrient-poor Martian soil fertilized with his own feces. He repairs spacesuit breaches and blown-out airlocks with duct tape. He even jury-rigs his own long-haul vehicle powered by solar batteries and warmed with radioactive plutonium, then treks to the landing site of NASA's real-life Pathfinder rover to reactivate its radio and reestablish communications with Earth.

There are several small inaccuracies in both Weir's book and Scott's film. The wind from a dust storm that initially strands the astronaut on Mars would in reality barely ripple a flag, because the Martian atmosphere is so thin. Instead of extracting water from rocket fuel, a real-life Watney might mine and purify water from deposits of ice thought to exist beneath the soil across large swaths of the planet. And because Mars' atmosphere and magnetic field are too insubstantial to shield against cosmic radiation, Watney's skittishness about warming himself with heavily shielded plutonium is misguided—in fact, most of his radiation exposure would come from simply walking around outside in his spacesuit.

But these are minor technical quibbles. *The Martian*'s greater divergences from reality are less about science, and more about technology and politics. The key question to ask about *The Martian*'s accuracy is this: Would Watney—or anyone else—even be on Mars in the first place for the story to unfold?

Neither the book nor the movie explicitly say when exactly the story takes place, but Weir (as well as clever readers who reverse-engineered the book's timeline) has revealed that Watney and his crewmates land on Mars in November 2035. They get there via a four-month voyage in a very large, very expensive interplanetary shuttle that cycles crews back and forth between Mars and Earth. The shuttle also spins to provide artificial gravity to its occupants, to protect them from the wasting caused by extended stays in zero gravity. Furthermore, Watney's mission is actually the third human landing on Mars, preceded by two landings earlier in the 2030s.

All this seems to mesh with NASA's "Journey to Mars" program, which aims to send astronauts to Mars in the 2030s. But a closer look at NASA's program reveals potential problems. Despite its scientific and technical accuracy, *The Martian* seems to take place in a fairy-tale world where NASA possesses much more political power—and has a far larger share of the federal budget than its current meager 0.4 percent.

NASA has no plans for a large, spinning cycler spacecraft between Earth and Mars, probably because such a spacecraft is considered unaffordable. In fact, ongoing squabbles in Washington over how to divvy up NASA's persistently flat budget means that essentially *all* the crucial components for the agency's planned voyages—the heavy-lift rockets, the power sources, engines and spacecraft for deep space, the landers, surface habitats and ascent vehicles—are behind schedule and still in early stages of development, if they are being developed at all. And the agency's Journey to Mars could all go away, very quickly, at the whim of some future President or Congressional majority. Mired in the muck of politics, NASA may not manage to land even one crew of astronauts on Mars by 2035—let alone three.

Then again, by the 2030s, there may be good reasons to avoid landing on Mars. The search for extraterrestrial life is arguably the most powerful motivation for sending humans to Mars—but also the very thing that could scuttle such missions. This week's announcement from NASA confirming transient flows of liquid water on present-day Mars is fueling a debate over whether humans could visit the Red Planet's most tantalizing and habitable regions without spoiling them. Earthly microbes have already hitchhiked on several robotic interplanetary voyages due to our less-than-perfect spacecraft sterilization techniques, carrying with them the risk of contaminating or destroying any native ecosystems where they land.

If rare, tenacious microbes on a robot are a problem, then the trillions living within each and every human explorer would be a far greater worry. A new report released last week from the National Academy of Sciences says such "planetary protection" concerns could limit human landings to the parts of Mars considered least likely to hold life. Those regions, it must be said, are shrinking as satellite imagery and robotic landers reveal ever-larger portions of the Martian environment as more hospitable than previously believed. If respected, such restrictions could make the politicians controlling NASA's budget wonder why we should bother sending humans to Mars at all.

One provisional solution to the problems of budgets and contamination, offered in a second report released this week by the Planetary Society, is to send humans not to Mars itself in the 2030s, but rather to its moons, the 20-kilometer-wide Phobos and its half-sized sibling, Deimos. Both moons are easy to visit because of their low surface gravities, and they are most likely littered with ancient debris that asteroid impacts blasted into orbit from the Martian surface. After those lunar sorties in the 2030s, humans might at last descend to Mars at the end of that decade and in the 2040s.

Because it defers the expensive, slow development of new technologies for landing and living on Mars, the plan could be cheaper and easier for NASA to accomplish by the 2030s within the constraints of its projected budget. And it would allow more time to solve the difficult problems of planetary protection—either through improved methods for quarantining humans on the surface, or, more ambitiously, through the use of advanced telerobotics. The round-trip lag time for messages between researchers on Earth and rovers on Mars averages around 20 minutes, limiting the efficiency, flexibility, and speed of exploration. The two-way communication time between Mars and its moon Phobos is just 40 milliseconds, making it possible to use entirely new classes of robotic explorers that have never before been deployed on other planets.

Instead of being stranded on Mars, by 2035 an astronaut like Watney might more realistically be found on a moon overhead, virtually exploring the Red Planet with remote-controlled robots that scale cliffs, spelunk into caverns, burrow into the ground and fly through the air. In time, *The Martian*'s portrayal of microbe-riddled astronauts huffing and puffing around Mars in bulky spacesuits may seem quaint. For now, go check out the film—it's the closest most of us will ever get to Mars for a long time. Which might not be a bad thing.

## About the Author

*Lee Billings is a senior editor for space and physics at* Scientific American.

# Is "Protecting" Mars from Contamination a Half-Baked Idea?

By Michael J. Battaglia

I magine sending paleontologists to the Olduvai Gorge to find evidence of hominin habitation, but to avoid at all costs venturing too close to any area that looks most promising for fossils.

This is roughly analogous to how NASA is approaching its recently announced confirmation of features on the Red Planet, likely evidence of flowing water. Called recurring slope lineae (RSL), these tracks created by water are reason for great excitement, especially because they are just the kind of formations that may be conducive to Martian biology.

Because one RSL is in range of the Curiosity rover, currently sniffing around Gale Crater, what should be a rare chance to follow up the discovery from orbit with in situ data instead creates a dilemma. NASA's Office of Planetary Protection has advised the rover might contaminate the possibly moist soil with surviving Earth life that may have hitched a ride on it, and its Planetary Science Division is pondering whether it should allow Curiosity to live up to its name and take a detour to directly examine the intriguing hotspot—or at least zap it with its laser from a safe distance.

The biennial International Council for Science's Committee on Space Research (COSPAR) Planetary Protection Policy report recently updated its protocols about avoiding contamination on Mars by humans and their machines. (The U.S. is also a signatory to the Outer Space Treaty of 1967 that forbids contamination of "the moon and celestial bodies.") The report classifies areas on Mars as "Special Regions" defined by their life-friendly conditions. (There are also "Uncertain Regions" that may later be found to hold some potential for breeding Earth critters.) These are bio-hotspots where water (liquid or ice), volcanism, caves, geothermal activity or methane concentrations are evident—in other words, every promising location where scientists might concentrate their searches for life.

Major discoveries such as evidence of flowing water have whet the public's imagination. Shying away from bio-hotspots, along with not equipping probes to directly look for life surely dampens this enthusiasm. It could also dilute the political will to continue funding the multibillion-dollar assault on our ruddy neighbor into the next decade with a fleet of orbiters and rovers that will probably continue to report back "exciting" revelations of ancient floods, probable liquid water and the potential for life that always seems to be in locations we avoid on the Red Planet.

Although well intentioned, cordoning off life-friendly regions is too restrictive, given the probably unachievable standard of exploring for Martian biology only when researchers are assured no Earthly contamination would be introduced. (There is also concern with Martian biology contaminating Earth after two-way missions.) To rest easy, should we just forget direct investigation and limit ourselves to geologically interesting areas like those Curiosity and upcoming surface spacecraft are slated to visit? If we are really serious about planetary purity, we should only use telescopes. (Even orbiters may eventually crash and release surviving spores they might carry.) Such a purist approach would be absurd and unscientific. But what about our current legal and self-imposed restrictions? Are they also too limiting, and at odds with NASA's long-term goals of sample-return and eventual human visitation?

Sad to say, it is a reasonable argument that unsterilized Curiosity should not directly investigate the nearby RSL without an assurance that it would not spread potential contamination beyond the site. (Although the rover is not equipped to directly search for life, it could add supporting evidence for the findings from orbit.)

Given the Red Planet's potential for extant life—and the impossibility of guaranteeing sterility—the report recommends that we tread lightly in our search. Yet, some researchers think the whole idea of planetary protection is a waste of money and time, given the transfer of material that has occurred between the planets over the millennia and the almost negligible likelihood that any surviving Earth microbes could expand and multiply over large areas in Mars's harsh environment.

Getting our equipment as clean as possible rather than designating areas on Mars off-limits seems like a more realizable way to keep any Earthly invaders from tangling with Martian beasties. But our current obsession with sterility makes the perfect the enemy of the good. Thanks to possible panspermia, we may never be certain any biology discovered on the Red Planet is native Martian life, unless it is something totally alien to our own DNA-based biology. And even if we don't find home-grown Martians, but rather life that could be Mars-evolved microbes or fossils traceable to Earth, transplanted millions of years ago, this would be an extremely important discovery, too.

Rather than quarantine biologically interesting areas, space agencies should prep and equip future probes so we don't have to continue skirting hotspots. Besides Scout landers and flyers, sample-return and deep drilling, NASA has proposed the Astrobiology Field Laboratory, which would be the first probe since Viking to directly look for life and possibly refire public enthusiasm. It would seem to make scientific sense to dispatch this and other life-searching rovers to accessible bio-hotspots after investing in and developing high-sterilization methods and other cleaning techniques to minimize false positives. It also is a good way to curtail contamination by sending easier-to-sterilize robotic life-searching rovers, landers and sample-return spacecraft before we plant germ-covered boots on our neighbor.

Relying on such measures doesn't mean we have to stop regulating Mars exploration by region, however. The COSPAR guidelines are not inflexible, rather they are set to evolve with our increasing data about conditions on Mars and growing knowledge about the limits of survival for Earth microbes. Some Special Regions could remain off-limits, to be pristine forever. Others could sequentially be opened as we improve sterilization methodology and equipment. Of course, this may be more easily said than done, because we still have to learn how conducive Mars's environment would be to transferring biological material between explored and protected regions.

The current restrictions serve us now but may inhibit future scientific inquiry and exploration. Opening Mars to more thorough robotic investigation should be done in an orderly way, and with the caveat that perfectly controlled laboratory conditions are not possible. Of course, it would be great to robotically find life before we face a new dilemma when the biggest contaminants of all—astronauts—press their boot prints into the possibly vital Martian soil.

*The views expressed are those of the author(s) and are not necessarily those of Scientific American.*

## About the Author

*Michael J. Battaglia is Scientific American's Senior Online Copy Editor.*

# Can Mars Be Terraformed?

## By Christopher Edwards and Bruce Jakosky

People have long thought about converting Mars from the cold, dry planet it is today to one that would be inhabitable by humans. This notion of "terraforming" Mars has been popular for decades in science fiction and popular media—including, for example, several of the *Star Trek* movies and television episodes. In some sense, the idea of a terraformed Mars harkens back to the time when Percival Lowell postulated that Mars was inhabited by Martians, using giant canals to transport water from the Martian polar caps to the equator to save a dying civilization.

Is terraforming Mars feasible today? Is there enough $CO_2$ locked up in the planet that, if it could be mobilized back into the atmosphere, would create a thicker atmosphere and a warmer environment? We have used spacecraft measurements from the last 20 years to estimate how much $CO_2$ remains on the planet and recently published a paper in *Nature Astronomy* that assessed how much of the remaining $CO_2$ can be released with present-day technology. We didn't address what technology might be used, but Elon Musk has suggested, for example, that we could terraform Mars simply by exploding nuclear bombs over the polar caps. The heat from those would release the $CO_2$ locked up in the polar caps back into the atmosphere, and the thicker atmosphere would produce greenhouse warming to heat the planet.

Before we reveal the answer, a bit of background:

Today, we know that Mars is not inhabited by Martians, although it's possible that there could be microbes living underground. More than 50 years of robotic missions, mostly by NASA and the European Space Agency, have revealed an understanding of the planet's once-strong-but-now-miniscule magnetic field; evidence of huge river channels and precipitation-created valley networks; standing lakes; and a complicated evolution of the polar caps. These and other discoveries have changed our understanding of the Martian environment and caused a dramatic reconsideration by the planetary science community of Mars as a dynamic planet with a complex history.

In our study, we found that much of the planet's $CO_2$ has been lost to space, and that very little of what remains can be put back into the atmosphere. Mars' current atmospheric pressure is approximately six millibars (mbar), or just over one half of one percent of the pressure at the surface of the Earth. $CO_2$ is present as ice in the polar caps; as gas "adsorbed" (or physically bonded) to regolith grains; as carbon-bearing minerals (carbonates) either in the shallow regolith or deep within the crust; and possibly as "clathrates," which consist of water molecules forming a solid with a cage-like, open structure in which a "guest" molecule such as $CO_2$ can reside. The total amount of gas present in these reservoirs is likely to be less than the equivalent of some 100 mbar (as an equivalent pressure if it were all released into the atmosphere) and maybe only about 20 mbar of it could be readily put into the atmosphere. This falls well short of the one bar atmosphere of $CO_2$ that would be needed to warm the planet enough to allow liquid water to be stable.

The scale of the task of terraforming Mars becomes truly daunting if we consider the massive amounts of $CO_2$ that humans have poured into our own atmosphere through the burning of fossil fuels. Orders of magnitude more $CO_2$ are needed than that released by the entirety of humanity throughout history. It would take the equivalent of a million $CO_2$ icebergs a kilometer across to terraform Mars.

There may be ways to do it without a lot of $CO_2$, such as by manufacturing and releasing greenhouse gases with a much higher heat-trapping efficiency. That activity has to be far in the future, however, as we haven't even sent a first human expedition to Mars. For the foreseeable future, at least, any humans that do go to Mars will be using spacesuits and enclosed habitats to explore the red planet, much as we did for the human exploration of the moon in the late 1960s and early 1970s.

Perhaps humanity's greatest resource is the imagination of its people. This imagination can be articulated by visionaries such as scientists, entrepreneurs, inventors or world leaders—individuals who can see beyond our current limitations to a new and different future. For outer space, their science fiction serves as a guide to a future where humans are not limited to our own planet, space travel is routine and distant, and fantastic adventures await. As technology continues to revolutionize our everyday lives, science fiction may become reality, and our current problems with terraforming Mars may be looked upon like a telegraph wire in the time of the smartphone.

*The views expressed are those of the author(s) and are not necessarily those of Scientific American.*

## About the Authors

*Christopher Edwards is an Assistant Professor of Planetary Science in the Department of Physics and Astronomy at Northern Arizona University who uses satellite data to understand the composition, physical properties and morphology of the ancient Martian surface.*

*Bruce Jakosky is a Professor in the Laboratory for Atmospheric and Space Physics and the Department of Geological Sciences at the University of Colorado, and is the Principal Investigator for the MAVEN spacecraft mission currently orbiting Mars.*

# Aerogel Mars

By Caleb A. Scharf

B ack in July 2019 an intriguing paper appeared in the journal *Nature Astronomy*. The article reports on a study undertaken by Wordsworth, Kerber, and Cockell to investigate what might happen if you plastered parts of Mars with a thin, two to three centimeter layer of silica aerogel.

The background motivation for this work (which included both experiments here on Earth and mathematical modeling) was to ask whether there are alternative ways to imagine terraforming Mars—making it more suitable for life such as exists on Earth.

There are many challenges for terrestrial organisms on Mars: There is only a thin, carbon dioxide dominated atmosphere. Consequently fierce, molecule damaging ultra-violet radiation from the Sun reaches down to the martian surface. Mars is also very dry on its surface, although there is substantial water locked into subsurface deposits, most of which may be frozen. Mars has a caustic mix of chemistry in its soil-like regolith, including nasty stuff like ammonium perchlorate (sometimes used as solid rocket fuel here on Earth). And Mars gets cold, particularly at night and during the winter months in either hemisphere.

In principle, as traditional ideas about terraforming suggest, if you could thicken up Mars's atmosphere you could help with a lot of these challenges. One option might be to try to unleash the huge reserves of frozen $CO_2$ currently locked into the polar caps. But the scale of this operation puts it a long way off as a practical option. Plus, of course, there are valid questions about the whole notion of changing a pristine natural environment (which may still contain extant organisms, until proven otherwise) just because we want to.

As an alternative, what Wordsworth et al. suggest is a kind of localized "farming" approach. Silica aerogel is extremely low density and porous, but it can also produce a solid-state greenhouse effect because it's fairly opaque to infrared radiation (and doesn't conduct heat well) but is partially transparent to visible and shorter wavelength light.

The bottom line is that if aerogel was placed over a region of ice-rich regolith on Mars (towards the poles for instance), within a decade the solid-state greenhouse effect could warm the land down to many meters depth. The silica would also block the most destructive UV light. The temperatures could climb into a range where, underground at least, liquid water could occur for much of the year. In this kind of environment, with light still reaching the surface, we could imagine photosynthetic microbes getting a foothold. Especially if the aerogel layer is lightly airtight, maintaining a slightly higher atmospheric pressure beneath it.

Of course, whether terrestrial (or indeed indigenous organisms, if they have ever existed on Mars) would survive and thrive is highly uncertain. Nutrient flow would be needed, and the silica aerogel would have to be manufactured on an industrial scale. The authors do point out that tiny marine diatoms on Earth are already good little silica engineers—building amorphous silica particles. Perhaps synthetic biology could be developed to build its own greenhouse covering on Mars.

Maybe the most interesting aspect of the study is how it shifts the idea of terraforming Mars to, in a sense, local "farming" of Mars. The impact on the global state of the planet could be kept to a minimum, while the natural resources are sustainably utilized. Indeed, by keeping most of the planet in its natural, desolate state, the odds of catastrophic ecological change might be significantly reduced. And in the end it might be better to aerogel parts of the planet to grow food than to build colossal biosphere-like tents and all of their attendant infrastructure.

*The views expressed are those of the author(s) and are not necessarily those of Scientific American.*

## About the Author

*Caleb A. Scharf is director of astrobiology at Columbia University. He is author and co-author of more than 100 scientific research articles in astronomy and astrophysics. His work has been featured in publications such as* New Scientist, Scientific American, Science News, Cosmos Magazine, Physics Today *and* National Geographic. *For many years he wrote the* Life, Unbounded *blog for* Scientific American.

# Surviving Mars

By Caleb A. Scharf

The last piece I wrote here, "Death on Mars", sure got a conversation going. In a vigorous flurry of commentary on social media I was cast as either a voice of reason or a total pariah for daring to suggest that certain bold ideas for Mars exploration might face some rather nasty roadblocks. Why roadblocks? Because physics. Because biology.

As I explained in that piece, I am actually very enthusiastic about the remarkable advances being made in the space-launch industry. But if we're going to take ideas like the large-scale human settlement of Mars seriously (putting aside reasonable concerns about our priorities while Earth is undergoing changes that challenge humanity) we need to have a longer conversation and to take some care over our enthusiasm. *If only to ensure that when failures do occur we don't give up because our expectations were too high and too unrealistic.*

In that spirit (not to be taken as a rigorous analysis, but as some points to think about) here are some further questions about a human presence on Mars:

**Q: It may be bad but the surface of Mars is more hospitable than the Moon or Venus, right?**

**A:** In many respects this is true. There is a modest atmosphere, so you're not contending with absolute vacuum. Or such extreme temperature variations as on the Moon. Or the crushing pressures on Venus. Although, at around 0.7% of Earth's sea-level pressure, any on-foot exploration of Mars would require a full pressure suit of some form. That's to both stop your body from swelling and hemorrhaging in nasty ways, but to also make sure that enough oxygen is driven into your bloodstream.

Even if pressurized to about 1/3rd of Earth's surface pressure (like current NASA "soft" EMU suits in low-Earth orbit) that means you need a close-to-100% oxygen atmosphere in the suit, and will contend with a "pre-breathe" protocol to prevent decompression sickness where nitrogen bubbles form in your body. On the ISS, NASA's pre-breathe sessions can run from 4-12 hours depending on the protocols followed for a spacewalk. In other words, you're not going to be quickly popping your suit on for an after-dinner stroll on Mars, unless you stay in a low pressure, high oxygen environment all the time (with increased hazards for fires) or have high pressure suits–which are certainly under development.

The low pressure, very dry martian atmosphere also means that volatile substances tend to boil or sublimate very quickly. Solid or liquid water exposed at low latitudes on Mars (where temperatures are more moderate) will turn to vapor quite fast. There's no hauling chunks of polar water ice back to camp unless you seal them in an airtight container. There will also be constraints on any kind of adhesives, sealants, and other materials that you allow to be exposed to the raw environment (also because of UV damage from sunlight, which is significant).

**Q: A third of Earth's surface gravitational acceleration sounds pretty good though?**

**A:** On the face of it perhaps. You'd feel buoyant, lighter, with less effort to move your body. But we really don't know what 0.37g does to a human body over time. We have good data on the extremes: 1g and micro (or zero) g. We know that micro-g is challenging and requires a lot of effort to stave off the worst of the physiological effects: from dramatic bone density loss (and kidney stress as all that calcium tries exit your system), to cardiovascular changes, immediate and prolonged epigenetic changes, and vision impairment possibly related to increased cerebrospinal fluid in the brain's ventricles (which may also have cognitive impacts). Medication regimes could help, but they might be regimes for life if you stay on Mars. And that means either reliance on Earth's pharmaceutical supply or extensive in-house production.

There have also been experiments simulating the simple effect of lower gravity on human walking speed. Because of the nature of our anatomy and gait it appears that on Mars we might weigh less but we would only be able to comfortably walk at about half our normal pace. Martian Olympics might not be so very exciting.

**Q: But Mars has great natural resources for living off the land right?**

**A:** It does. Mars has a huge amount of water in total (in subsurface ice and bonded in ordinary regolith), and it's got a surface mineral composition that's pretty familiar in many ways. It receives a decent amount of solar electromagnetic radiation–roughly 60% of the power per square meter on Mars compared to a similar site on Earth. And towards the polar regions are vast deposits of frozen carbon dioxide. The problem is getting your hands on any of this in the first place.

Take the regolith (soil). Data from the Curiosity rover suggests that, by mass, 1-3% of regolith is water. So, in principle, cooking up regolith to release that water and then condensing it could provide a practical supply. There are caveats though.

For one thing, if you wanted to use this water for growing your food au naturel (like potatoes, for instance), martian soil sucks. That's because it is actually toxic due to chlorine-containing compounds called perchlorates. Earth-based experiments on plants exposed to the level of perchlorates on Mars indicate that most species suffer. Those that are resistant end up with high perchlorate concentrations in their structures. You don't want to eat that.

There are terrestrial microbes that actually consume perchlorates (since they're energy-rich oxidants) and are already used to help clean contaminated water on Earth. So farming on Mars would have to involve a lot of careful preparatory work to get rid of toxins in the water and soil, and to ensure a supply of the right nutrients (even in hydroponic growing). The larger the scale of food production the bigger the challenge.

And there's the rub for most of Mars's plentiful resources. They're going to need extensive and careful refining and purification, with the possible exception of brute force applications (like electrolysis of water to make oxygen and hydrogen). In all instances that requires a substantial energy budget. And before you forget: Having oxygen is not enough to keep humans happy, you also have to scrub the carbon dioxide from the air that we exhale or we die–involving more energy use and materials, and possibly a critical role for plant life on Mars.

**Q: We'll just end up terraforming Mars, that'll be the real solution?**
**A:** It could be, if we really knew how to accomplish such a thing beyond back-of-the-envelope theorizing. I've written about that before on these pages. It would require engineering on a scale exceeding anything that we've attempted before. It would even exceed the scale of our unintentional influence on the carbon dioxide concentration of Earth's atmosphere over the past couple of centuries.

We could heat up the martian polar zones (perhaps using orbital mirrors), releasing the frozen carbon dioxide to thicken the atmosphere. We could bring in comets and ammonia to boost the greenhouse effect and build a nitrogen rich chemical buffer in the atmosphere. We could try to engineer microbes capable of transforming the soil chemistry and adding molecules to the atmosphere.

But we might not be able to predict all of the outcomes. If any of this engineering really worked we'd have a new planet, with new climate zones and atmospheric circulation (cyclones, tornadoes, precipitation after billions of years of drought) that would, by the very nature of these things, be unpredictable and tricky. What if terraforming simply makes Mars into a maelstrom-ridden hell?

**Q: What next then?**

**A:** This list could go on. The point is not to reject any of our ideas about putting people on Mars, or even establishing the kind of existential hedge-fund that folk like Elon Musk are talking about, or to prematurely dismiss the kind of expansionist (and rather anachronistic) view of what our species should do with itself in the future. All are worth discussing and perhaps doing something about. But don't kid yourself into thinking that we either know how to really do any of this, or that it won't kill a lot of people in the process. Figuring out the details is key. The best kind of journey is often one that is well prepared for.

*The views expressed are those of the author(s) and are not necessarily those of* Scientific American.

## About the Author

*Caleb A. Scharf is director of astrobiology at Columbia University. He is author and co-author of more than 100 scientific research articles in astronomy and astrophysics. His work has been featured in publications such as* New Scientist, Scientific American, Science News, Cosmos Magazine, Physics Today *and* National Geographic. *For many years he wrote the* Life, Unbounded *blog for* Scientific American.

# How to Grow Vegetables on Mars

By Edward Guinan, Scott Engle, and Alicia Eglin

This may not be the right time to bring this up, but let's just say it: there's strong reason to believe illnesses like COVID-19 might become more prevalent in coming years. When we encroach on previously untouched areas—such as wild lands, dense jungles and tropical forests—we unleash unknown viruses that our bodies have no protection against. As the human population grows and natural habitats shrink, this cycle will likely continue. Other catastrophic dangers to Earth include collisions with asteroids and comets, global thermonuclear or biochemical warfare, and of course the long-term effects of global warming.

To lessen these dangers, we might need to get away. Far away. Like all the way to Mars. The primary reasons for going are to explore and to search for life—both past and present. But settlements on Mars also provide a safe haven for humankind in the unlikely event that something catastrophic happens to the Earth. Going to Mars isn't just fanciful, pie-in-the-sky thinking. NASA is under presidential orders to land humans on Mars by 2033, and the organization is studying ways to build human habitations on the Red Planet. In 2016, SpaceX publicly announced a comprehensive vision to begin building settlements on Mars, proposing a high-capacity transportation infrastructure. This two-phase mission could put people on Mars by 2026.

This potential colonization is why astrobiology students at Villanova began their Mars Gardens project, investigating which plants and vegetables can grow in iron oxide–rich Martian soil simulant (MSS). Over 45 different kinds of plants have been tested since the program began in 2017—and, given that these are college students, it's unsurprising that the tests included hops and barley.

Plants grown in potting mix under the same environmental conditions served as "controls," and the simulant regolith (soil) is based to a large extent on volcanic rock from the Mojave Desert. MSS, which tends to be denser, is available online and comes from

NASA's chemical analysis of Martian samples. However, the actual regolith on Mars contains perchlorates that are dangerous to humans. So, once on Mars, this hazardous chemical will have to be removed before the actual soil is used. Also, the sunlight on Mars is weaker, which affects growing conditions. So, the Villanova students took all the right steps to replicate Martian greenhouse conditions, and accounted for as many variables as possible—all with the goal of answering the question: Can plants be grown on Mars in Martian soil under reduced ambient light?

## The Unwelcoming Planet

Before we answer that, let's take a big-picture look at Mars. It's safe to say the environment there isn't exactly welcoming: Overall, Mars is small (about one 10th of Earth's mass), cold (on average, −50 degrees Celsius) and desolate. It has a very thin, carbon dioxide–rich atmosphere that's about one 90th as dense of Earth's. Mars is roughly 141 million miles from the sun (Earth is 93 million miles), meaning the maximum intensity of sunlight on Mars is about 43 percent the strength of the sunlight on Earth. There is some good news, however, as beneficial carbon dioxide and nitrogen make up about 95 percent and 2.6 percent of the planet's atmosphere, respectively. However, without any ozone in the Martian atmosphere, the greenhouse windows would need to block harmful solar ultraviolet radiation.

A few billion years ago, Mars boasted a more hospitable environment, complete with oceans, a temperate climate and—quite possibly—life. It has since lost most of its atmosphere and water inventories, and there is currently no water on its surface. Water (or ice) is present beneath the surface, however, as well as in the planet's icy polar regions. These harsh conditions make it necessary for all plants to be grown in heated, pressurized greenhouses with significant compensations made for atmosphere, humidity and water.

In their greenhouse experiments, the Villanova students took strenuous measures to create an environment that's both plant-friendly and similar to what would be found in greenhouses on Mars. They ensured, for instance, that plants received roughly the same amount of sunlight as they would on Mars. Given these requirements, the students also experimented with growing some plants hydroponically.

The students found that their success rates could be improved with two enhancements: augmenting sunlight by using multiwavelength LEDs and loosening the dense MSS by adding potting soil—or earthworm feces.

Based on all these factors, students were able to eliminate certain vegetables from consideration. For instance, the low light on Mars does not lend itself well to growing plants that require full sun, which include favorites like tomatoes, beans, legumes, corn or many root plants. Carrots also don't make the cut, as they tend to come out stunted in the claylike MSS. Potatoes largely don't thrive in the simulant soil and low light conditions, but sweet potatoes do a little better.

The students found that dandelions would flourish on Mars and have significant benefits: they grow quickly, every part of the plant is edible, and they have high nutritional value. Other thriving plants include microgreens, lettuce, arugula, spinach, peas, garlic, kale and onions.

Conditions on Mars for humans, let alone farmers, are far from easy. The difficult planet certainly isn't a natural home for us, and growing sustenance there would be a complicated task. That said, it's not impossible, and it's comforting to know that we could develop and maintain our own sources of food on a distant landscape. The possibility of growing hops and barley doesn't hurt, either.

*The views expressed are those of the author(s) and are not necessarily those of Scientific American.*

## About the Authors

*Edward Guinan, Ph.D., is a professor of astronomy and astrophysics at Villanova University.*

*Scott Engle, Ph.D., is a professor of astronomy and astrophysics at Villanova University.*

*Alicia Eglin is a third-year undergraduate astronomy and astrophysics major at Villanova University; she has been working on the Mars Gardens project since 2018.*

# Section 3: Searching for Martian Life

3.1   Water Flows on Mars Today, NASA Announces
      By Clara Moskowitz

3.2   Searching for Life in Martian Water Will Be Very, Very Tricky
      By Lee Billings

3.3   The Search for Life on Mars Is About to Get Weird
      By Leonard David

3.4   Curiosity Rover Uncovers Long-Sought Organic Materials
      on Martian Surface
      By Adam Mann

3.5   Deep within Mars, Liquid Water Offers Hope for Life
      By Lee Billings

3.6   I'm Convinced We Found Evidence of Life on Mars in the 1970s
      By Gilbert V. Levin

3.7   Until Recently, People Accepted the "Fact" of Aliens in
      the Solar System
      By Caleb A. Scharf

# Water Flows on Mars Today, NASA Announces

## By Clara Moskowitz

The Red Planet is wet, scientists announced today. New evidence from NASA's Mars Reconnaissance Orbiter (MRO) confirms that suspicious dark streaks on Mars that appear and disappear with the seasons are created by flowing liquid water. The streaks are made by salty water that runs down steep hills during warm months, when temperatures are above –23 degrees Celsius, and freezes during colder times.

The intriguing streaks, called recurring slope lineae, were first spotted in 2010 in images from the MRO's HiRISE (High-Resolution Imaging Science Experiment) camera. Scientists have long suspected that the streaks marked the location of liquid water. Now researchers have found the chemical signatures of hydrated minerals on these slopes, confirming that explanation. The new evidence also comes from the MRO via CRISM, its Compact Reconnaissance Imaging Spectrometer for Mars, which separates light into its constituent wavelengths to reveal the chemicals present on the Martian surface. The instrument saw the signatures of magnesium perchlorate, magnesium chlorate and sodium perchlorate—all hydrated salts that require water to form and also contain it. The chemicals appear in the summer, when the dark streaks are visible, and disappear along with the features when temperatures drop. "This is the best evidence of liquid water on Mars in the present day," says Georgia Institute of Technology scientist James Wray, co-author of a paper reporting the data published today in *Nature Geoscience*. "The fact that these chemicals are sitting on these flows and concentrated there and have water means there's really no way that water wasn't involved." (*Scientific American* is part of Nature Publishing Group.)

The findings provide yet more evidence that Mars is not a dry and barren landscape but rather a dynamic place that changes with the seasons—and, just maybe, holds the ingredients necessary for life. Primary among those ingredients, of course, is water, which makes the recurring slope lineae a prime spot to search for signs of extraterrestrial microbes.

Wray says the new evidence for water is an encouraging development in the search for life, but he points out that there is much we still don't know—"how deep the water goes, how low the temperature gets and how high the salt concentration gets. We need to characterize those aspects of the water to really be able to answer the question [of habitability]. But at least we know where to look now."

The recurring slope lineae, most of which are roughly a few meters wide and tens to hundreds of meters long, are common throughout the planet's equator and mid-latitudes. "These features are very sensitive to temperature," Alfred McEwen, principal investigator for the HiRISE camera at the University of Arizona in Tucson, said Monday during a NASA press conference announcing the results. "They form at different times and different latitudes on Mars, all related to the seasonal variations at those locations. The darkening can be explained if these are seeps of water that seep through the shallow surface layer and darken the surface layer." The hydrated minerals indicate the water there is briny and the salts allow it to stay liquid in colder temperatures than would otherwise be possible. The Martian polar ice caps also contain water, but it is frozen and therefore would be less useful to living organisms.

Finding water on Mars is important not only because it might point to the presence of life on the Red Planet—it is also helpful for sending humans there. "Any resources Mars may have that we don't have to launch off Earth and take with us would help a lot," Wray says. "Finding places where water is present and not just in the form of ice up at the poles is useful for planning future exploration." Ironically, however, the very evidence of possible habitability that makes human exploration more appealing also makes it more fraught. According to a new joint review from the National Academy of Sciences and the European Science Foundation, NASA cannot in good conscience send manned missions to the Red Planet that

75

might contaminate native organisms with terrestrial bacteria. "We clean the spacecraft as best as we can but we know that microbial life, bacteria, are so tenacious that it's impossible to kill them all," John Grunsfeld, NASA's associate administrator for the Science Mission Directorate, said during the press conference. If NASA plans to send any mission near the recurring slope lineae, he added, scientists would carefully study the potential to contaminate Mars and take steps to prevent it. Before we can search Mars for life, in other words, we have to improve our ability to control hitchhiking Earthlings.

## About the Author

*Clara Moskowitz is Scientific American's senior editor covering space and physics. She has a bachelor's degree in astronomy and physics from Wesleyan University and a graduate degree in science journalism from the University of California, Santa Cruz. Follow Moskowitz on Twitter @ClaraMoskowitz.*

# Searching for Life in Martian Water Will Be Very, Very Tricky

## By Lee Billings

N ASA scientists announced today the best evidence yet that Mars, once thought dry, sterile and dead, may yet have life in it: Liquid water still flows on at least some parts of the Red Planet, seeping from slopes to accumulate in what might be life-nurturing pools at the bases of equatorial hills and craters. These remarkable sites on Mars may be the best locations in the solar system to search for extant extraterrestrial life—but doing so will be far from easy.

Examining potentially habitable regions of Mars for signs of life is arguably the primary scientific justification for sending humans there—but according to a new joint review from the National Academy of Sciences and the European Science Foundation, we are not presently prepared to do so.

The problem is not exploding rockets, shrinking budgets, political gamesmanship or fickle public support—all the usual explanations spaceflight advocates offer for the generations-spanning lapse in human voyages anywhere beyond low Earth orbit. Rather, the problem is life itself—specifically, the tenacity of Earthly microbes, and the potential fragility of Martian ones. The easiest way to find life on Mars, it turns out, may be to import bacteria from Cape Canaveral—contamination that could sabotage the search for native Martians. The need to protect any possible Martian biosphere from Earthly contamination, the review's authors wrote, could "prevent humans from landing in or entering areas" where Martian life might thrive. Although this sentiment is not new, its frank, formal acknowledgement in such an authoritative study is rare indeed. NASA is planning to send humans to Mars as soon as the 2030s; that such missions may unavoidably pose extreme contamination risks is understandably not something the agency is eager to highlight, even as it actively researches possible solutions to the problem.

Historically, in the context of Mars such "planetary protection" has primarily concerned robotic exploration. The risk of contamination is an issue even for machines, which, unlike humans, can endure being fried with radiation and bathed in harsh chemicals prelaunch to eradicate bacterial stowaways. Microbes that stubbornly refuse to die nonetheless turn up with regularity in NASA's supposedly sterile clean rooms for preparing interplanetary spacecraft. Apollo astronauts even found bacteria on the moon that had survived an almost total vacuum inside the robotic Surveyor 3 lander that had touched down more than two and a half years earlier. If terrestrial microbes could live in places like that, why not in some of the more habitable parts of Mars?

The United Nations Outer Space Treaty of 1967 forbids the "harmful contamination" of other worlds with Earth's biology, and an international organization called COSPAR (the Committee on Space Research) sets the planetary protection protocols for the U.S., Europe, Russia and other signatory spacefaring nations to follow. To protect Mars, since 2002 COSPAR has designated restricted "Special Regions" on the planet where conditions are warm and wet enough to possibly support extant Martian life—or to allow Earthly invaders to gain a flagella-hold. Because of rapid, ongoing progress in our knowledge of the Martian environment and the fundamental limits of Earthly biology, the precise definitions for Special Regions remain works in progress that are officially revisited every two years. The new joint review, released last week, recommends revisions to the findings of a 2014 report on COSPAR's Special Regions from NASA's Mars Exploration Program Analysis Group.

The closer planetary scientists look at Mars, the more Special Regions they think they see. Special Regions pepper the planet's equator and mid-latitudes, in eroded gullies and in steep, rocky slopes of hills and craters, where new evidence published September 28 in *Nature Geoscience* indicates that briny water flows and pools from aquifers during Martian summers. Special Regions can also be found in caves, beneath the polar ice caps and in geothermal hotspots of seismic or volcanic activity. As little as five meters below the surface, where groundwater may persist as ice, vast areas of the planet could be considered a Special Region, just waiting to be transformed into a welcoming, watery microbial Eden by the heat from a new-formed impact crater or the operations of a recently arrived spacecraft. Special Regions should also exist, the new review notes, at the still-unknown sources of mysterious methane emissions recently detected on Mars. On Earth it is generated chiefly by microbes but detectable quantities of the gas could also arise on Mars from abiotic sources, although those lifeless production routes would also require liquid water.

But knowing for certain whether any of these places are actually special probably requires visiting them—something that is very difficult to do under current protocols. Before a spacecraft can visit a Special Region it must in part or in whole be stringently sterilized according to strict rules, potentially adding years of development time and many millions of dollars onto a mission's bottom line. Even then, the protocols may not be strict enough—current techniques are incapable of entirely cleansing a spacecraft of microbes, and no one really knows the threshold conditions for bacteria to create viable, self-sustaining colonies on Mars—or on Earth, for that matter.

The agency's first—and to date only—missions to Mars explicitly in search of life were the twin Viking landers, which landed on the Red Planet in 1976. All others since have focused on finding signs of life from Mars' ancient past rather than its present. If even sterilized robots cannot be trusted to venture into Special Regions, what about microbe-riddled humans? If astronauts shall only be allowed to visit subpar locales to search for life on Mars, can NASA or any other entity justify the tens to hundreds of billions of dollars required to send them there? If a human crew lands in an area thought unpromising for biology but discovers habitable conditions or something living there, would they have to immediately relocate, or even pack up their rocket and launch back to orbit? These and other unanswered questions show how in many ways, discovering a present-day Martian biosphere could be both the realization of NASA's wildest dream and its worst nightmare. They explain as nothing else can the otherwise inexplicable fact that in the quest for extant life on Mars NASA has been judiciously avoiding the very places where it may most likely be found.

Carl Sagan famously mused that if life is ever found on the fourth rock from the sun, "Mars then belongs to the Martians, even if the Martians are only microbes." In this view the planet would become a sacrosanct sanctuary, forever off-limits to encroaching humans. An alternate perspective holds that planetary protection efforts are futile, perhaps even naive: Thanks to likely contamination from earlier spacecraft, as well as ancient exchanges of material blasted between the planets by massive asteroid impacts, Mars has probably already experienced many waves of Earthly invaders—each of which could have been easily repulsed by any native, more adaptively fit biosphere.

Amid all the uncertainty, the new review notes, one thing is very clear: "The planetary protection implications of sending astronauts to Mars raises profound questions at the intersection of science, engineering, technology, project management and public policy." The statement's true meaning for NASA and other space agencies should be equally clear: Although inconvenient, the planetary protection issues associated with crewed missions to Mars are too severe to be dismissed, dodged or downplayed. Now is the time to begin addressing them. Otherwise, human voyages there may at best prove to be nonstarters and at worst become fiascos that forever extinguish hopes of studying pristine examples of Martian life.

## About the Author

*Lee Billings is a senior editor for space and physics at* Scientific American.

# The Search for Life on Mars Is About to Get Weird

By Leonard David

Mesa, Arizona—Since the dawn of the space age NASA and other agencies have spent billions of dollars to reconnoiter Mars—assailing it with spacecraft flybys, photo-snapping orbiters and landers nose-diving onto its surface. The odds are good, many scientists say, for the Red Planet being an extraterrestrial address for alien life—good enough to sustain decades' worth of landing very expensive robots to ping it with radar, zap it with lasers, trundle across its terrain and scoop up its dirt. Yet against all odds (and researchers' hopes for a watershed discovery), Mars remains a poker-faced world that holds its cards tight. No convincing signs of life have emerged. But astrobiologists continue to, quite literally, chip away at finding the truth.

As the search becomes more heated (some would say more desperate), scientists are entertaining an ever-increasing number of possible explanations for Martian biology as a no-show. For example, could there be a "cover up" whereby the harsh Martian environment somehow obliterates all biosignatures—all signs of past or present life? Or perhaps life there is just so alien its biosignatures are simply unrecognizable to us, hidden in plain view.

Of course, the perplexing quest to find life on Mars may have a simple solution: It's not there, and never was. But as the proceedings of this year's Astrobiology Science Conference held here in April made clear, life-seeking scientists are not giving up yet. Instead, they are getting more creative, proposing new strategies and technologies to shape the next generation of Mars exploration.

## A Slumbering Biosphere?

Talk about looking for Martians and you inevitably talk about water, the almost-magical liquid that sustains all life on Earth and seems to have served as an indispensable kick-starter for biology in our planet's deepest past. "It all started out with 'follow the water;' not necessarily 'follow the life'...but 'follow one of the basic requirements for living systems,'" says Arizona State University geologist Jack Farmer, referring to NASA's oft-repeated mantra for Martian exploration. "There are many indications of water on Mars in the past, perhaps reservoirs of water in the near subsurface as well," he says. "But what is the quality of that water? Is it really salty—too salty for life?"

Without liquid water, Farmer points out, one would naively think organisms cannot function. The reality may be more complex: on Earth, some resilient organisms such as tardigrades can enter a profound, almost indefinite state of hibernation when deprived of moisture, preserving their desiccated tissues but neither growing nor reproducing. It is possible, Farmer says, that Martian microbes could spend most of their time as inert spores "waiting for something good to happen," only springing to life given the right and very rare conditions. Certain varieties of Earthly "extremophiles"—microbes that live at extremes of temperature, pressure, salinity and so on—exhibit similar behavior.

Farmer says there is as yet no general consensus about the best way to go about life detection on the Red Planet. This is due in no small part to the runaway pace of progress in biotechnology, which has led to innovations such as chemistry labs shrunken down to fit on a computer chip. These technologies "have been revolutionizing the medical field, and have now started to enter into concepts for life detection on Mars," he explains. Things move so fast that today's best technology for finding Martian biology may be tomorrow's laughably obsolete dead-end.

But no matter how sophisticated a lab on a chip might be, it won't deliver results if it is not sent to the right place. Farmer suspects that seriously seeking traces of life requires deep drilling on Mars. "I basically think we're going to have to gain access to the subsurface and look for the fossil record," he explains. But discovering a clear, unambiguous fossil biosignature on Mars would also raise a red flag. "We probably would approach the future of Mars exploration—particularly accessing habitable zones of liquid water in the deep subsurface—more cautiously, because life could still be there. So planetary protection would be taken very seriously," he says. ("Planetary protection" is the term scientists commonly use for precautions to minimize the chance of biological contamination between worlds. Think of it not so much in terms of bug-eyed aliens running rampant on Earth but of billion-dollar robots finding "Martians" that prove to only be hardy bacterial hitchhikers imported from our own world).

## The Martian Underground

Like-minded about deep diving on Mars is Penelope Boston, director of the NASA Astrobiology Institute at the agency's Ames Research Center. "That's my bias," she says. "Given Mars' current state, with all the challenging surface manifestations of dryness, radiation and little atmosphere, the best hope for life still extant on Mars is subsurface." The subsurface, she says, might also offer better chances of preserving past life—that is, of fossils, even if only of single-celled organisms.

The planet's depths hold the potential for harboring liquid water under certain circumstances, Boston thinks. But how far down might that water be? "I suspect it's pretty far...and how we get to it, that's a whole other kettle of fish," she says. Over the years scientists have estimated the average depth of the planet's possible liquid reservoirs as anywhere between tens of meters to kilometers. Then again, recent observations from orbiters have revealed mysterious dark streaks that seasonally flow down the sunlit sides of some Martian hillsides and craters. These "recurring slope lineae" could conceivably be brines of liquid water fed by aquifers very close to the surface, some researchers say.

83

Such lingering uncertainties emerge from the indirect and scattered nature of our studies of Mars, and ensure that any argument for life there is based solely on circumstantial information, Boston notes. "Each individual piece of evidence is, on its own merits, weak," she says. Only by amassing a diverse suite of independent measurements can a well-built case for life on Mars be made, she says: "In my opinion, we can't make that strong case unless we push to do all of those measurements on exactly the same precise spot. We don't do that because it's very difficult, but it's something to aspire to." Despite decades of sending costly hardware to Mars, Boston believes that what is still missing is a sense of harmony between instruments, allowing them to work together to support a search for alien life. "I think that the precise requirements of a really robust claim of life at the microscopic scale require us to push on further," she notes.

Attendees at the astrobiology meeting in Arizona showcased an assortment of high-tech devices for next-generation exploration, ranging from microfluidic "life analyzers" and integrated nucleic acid extractors for studying "Martian metagenomics" to exquisitely sensitive, miniaturized organic chemistry labs for spotting tantalizing carbon compounds and minerals at microscopic scales. Missing from the mix, however, was any solid consensus on how these and other tools could all work together to provide a slam-dunk detection of life on Mars.

## What's the Weather?

Some scientists contend a new kind of focus is sorely needed. Perhaps the pathway to finding any Martians lurking in the planet's nooks and crannies is to learn where exactly on Mars those potentially life-nurturing niches exist, and how they change over the course of days, months and years rather than over eons of geologic time. That is, to find homes for extant life on Mars today, researchers should probably not just be studying the planet's long-term climate but also its day-to-day weather.

"Right now we're sort of shifting gears. Once you've found out that a planet is habitable, then the next question is, 'Was there life?'—so it's a completely different ball game," says Nathalie Cabrol, director of the Carl Sagan Center at the SETI Institute. "On Mars you cannot look for life with the tools that have been looking for habitability of that planet," she argues. "We should be looking for habitats and not habitable environments. You are dealing on Mars with what I call extremophile extreme environments on steroids," she says, "and you don't look for microbial life with telescopes from Mars orbit."

Cabrol advocates making an unprecedentedly robust, high-resolution study of environmental variability on Mars by peppering its surface with weather stations. Sooner or later telltale signs of the possible whereabouts of extant life may emerge from the resulting torrents of data. "Today's environment on that planet is a reflection of something in the past," she says, and planting numbers of automated stations on Mars does not need to be expensive. "This is of interest not only to astrobiology but to human exploration. The first thing you want to know is what the weather is like," she says, adding, "Right now we're not equipped to do this and I'm not saying it's going to be easy to look for extant life. I'm not saying what we're doing now is wrong. Whatever we put on the ground we are learning. But there is variability on Mars. You go up or down one meter, things change. Habitats at a microscopic level can happen at the scale of a slope. It can happen at the scale of a rock!"

## Might *We* Be Martians?

"I think Mars offers us the highest chance of finding life" somewhere beyond Earth, says Dirk Schulze-Makuch, a planetary scientist at Technical University of Berlin in Germany. But, like Boston and others, he maintains confirmation of life will only come from multiple "layers of proof" that have to be consistent with one another. "We really need at least four different kinds of methods," he says. "My point is that there's no slam-dunk. We need several instruments. You have to build a case, and right now we can do better...unless the biosignature through a microscope is waving hello." The trouble, he adds, is that too-stringent planetary protection rules may preclude getting the evidence necessary for that proof. "We have the technology to go to places where there could be life," he says. "But we can't go to certain areas on Mars, like recurring slope lineae or...under patches of ice. It seems to be ridiculous."

Indeed, Schulze-Makuch speculates planetary protection may be a lost cause for Mars—or at least a misguided endeavor. It may even be that any Martian microbes are actually Earth's long-lost cousins. Or, conversely, Mars rather than Earth is really the sole site of biogenesis in our solar system. Both scenarios are possible, considering that single-celled organisms can likely survive world-shattering impacts and the subsequent interplanetary voyages if embedded in ejected shards of rock that could fall elsewhere as meteorites. Innumerable impacts of this scale battered the solar system billions of years ago, potentially blasting biological material between neighboring worlds. On balance, Schulze-Makuch says, "the chances are higher that we are Martians."

## About the Author

*Leonard David is author of* Moon Rush: The New Space Race *(National Geographic, 2019) and* Mars: Our Future on the Red Planet *(National Geographic, 2016). He has been reporting on the space industry for more than five decades.*

# Curiosity Rover Uncovers Long-Sought Organic Materials on Martian Surface

By Adam Mann

Nearly six years into its survey of a site called Gale Crater on Mars, NASA's Curiosity rover has delivered what may be the biggest discovery yet in its quest for signs of habitability and life: Organic molecules are abundant in Red Planet rocks, and the simplest organic molecule, methane, seasonally blows through the thin Martian air. On Earth, such carbon-rich compounds are one of life's cornerstones.

Both discoveries emerged from Curiosity's Sample Analysis at Mars (SAM) instrument, a miniaturized chemistry lab and oven that roasts dollops of air, rock and soil to sniff out each sample's constituent molecules. Samples of ancient mudstone yielded a diversity of organic molecules in SAM's oven—and in a separate study, five years' worth of atmospheric samples gathered by SAM tracked fluctuating levels of methane that peaked in the Martian summer. The results are reported in a pair of papers published recently in *Science*.

Although tantalizing, the two findings remain far from definitive when it comes to past or present life on Mars. Methane is ubiquitous in places like the atmospheres of gas-giant planets. It can also arise from lifeless interactions between flowing water and hot rocks whereas other simple organic molecules are known to exist in some meteorites and interstellar gas clouds. "Short of taking a picture of a fossil in a rock on Mars, [finding life there] is extremely difficult to do scientifically," says Chris Webster, a chemist at NASA's Jet Propulsion Laboratory and lead author of the methane study.

## Mars's Missing Carbon

That Mars possesses organic molecules is not surprising. Like every planet in our solar system, it receives a steady rain of carbon-rich micrometeorites and dust from space. Yet when NASA's twin Viking probes landed on Mars in 1976, their studies suggested something startling: Martian soil, it seemed, contained less carbon than lifeless lunar rocks. "It was a big surprise," says Caroline Freissinet, an astrobiologist and co-author on Curiosity's mudstone study at the Atmosphere, Media, Spatial Observations Laboratory (LATMOS) in France. "It slowed down the whole Mars program, unfortunately." Ever since, scientists have ardently hunted for Mars's missing carbon—or at least an explanation for its absence. A crucial clue came in 2008, when NASA's Phoenix lander found perchlorate salts—highly reactive molecules containing chlorine—in soil samples near the Martian north pole. Combined with high-energy ultraviolet light and cosmic rays streaming in from space, perchlorates would destroy any organic material on the surface, leaving little to be seen by carbon-seeking landers and rovers. Perhaps, some researchers speculated, Mars's remaining organics—and thus any signs of past or present life—were locked away in its subsurface depths.

In 2015, however, Curiosity made the first tentative detection of organic molecules on Mars, finding evidence of chlorine-contaminated carbon compounds in soil samples heated to more than 800 degrees Celsius in SAM. But early into the rover's mission, researchers discovered that carbon-rich chemical reagents were leaking out of some of SAM's components, potentially contaminating nearby samples. To combat the contamination, the Curiosity team focused on finding more chlorine-containing organics, and limited subsequent SAM runs to temperatures between 200 and 400 degrees C.

In their new work the team checked to see what this restrictive process might have missed. After carefully accounting for background contamination from SAM, Freissinet and her colleagues baked 3-billion-year-old mudstone samples at over 500 degrees C, a temperature at which perchlorates should have fully burned away. In the ashes that remained they found thiophenes—relatively small and simple ringlike molecules containing both carbon and sulfur. The latter element, it is thought, came from a sulfur-rich mineral called jarosite that previous Curiosity investigations had revealed in 3.5-billion-year-old deposits in Gale Crater—laid down at a time when the crater was warm, wet and apparently habitable. The researchers suspect the thiophenes' carbon came from as-yet-unidentified larger organic molecules, which had been trapped and preserved inside the jarosite for perhaps billions of years.

Despite this latest discovery's patchwork nature, George Cody, a geochemist at the Carnegie Institution for Science who was not involved in the work, considers it an impressive step forward. The presence of these larger molecules, he says, hints at well-preserved reservoirs of carbon hidden at and just below the Martian surface—a prospect that bolsters the case for future missions to collect samples and return them to Earth. "If you can do this on Mars, imagine what you can do with analytical facilities available to us on Earth," he says.

## Methane Spikes and Changing Seasons

In the meantime Curiosity has undertaken what Webster calls "the most important measurements of Mars methane made to date." The carbon-containing gas is significant because most methane on Earth is produced by methanogen microbes, which are common in oxygen-poor environments. Methane is also quickly broken down by ultraviolet radiation, so any of the gas discovered on Mars was probably released recently. Using SAM, Webster and his colleagues have found a persistent background level of methane in the atmosphere above Gale Crater over the last five years of about 0.4 part per billion—a scarcely detectable trace, to be sure, but enough to pique astrobiologists' interest. Tellingly, the methane levels appear to periodically spike in time with Martian seasons, being about three times higher in the sunny summertime than in the darker, colder winter.

This periodicity is to Webster the most exciting part of his team's results. Previous research had seen evidence for sporadic methane plumes on Mars, but never seasonally recurring events.

"It's like having a problem with your car," he says. "If it doesn't repeat, you can't find out what it is." The methane, he and his colleagues speculate, could come from aquifers melting during the Martian summer, releasing water that flows over rocks deep underground to produce fresh gas. Or it could be ancient, belched out billions of years ago by geologic or biological processes and then trapped in matrices of ice and rock that unfreeze when warmed by the sun. And, of course, there is always the chance that Martian methanogens still slumber in the planet's subsurface even today, periodically awakening during clement periods to produce their gaseous calling-card.

Other scientists who did not take part in the research had mixed reviews on findings' significance in the search for life. Michael Mumma, an astrobiologist at NASA Goddard Space Flight Center, considers the measurements important and says they provide ground-truth evidence for his independent (and controversial) detections of Martian methane plumes, using Earth-based telescopes. But Marc Fries, a planetary scientist who curates the cosmic dust collection at NASA Johnson Space Center, takes a more skeptical view. He points out carbon-rich meteorites and dust could generate the reported amounts of methane as they fell into the Martian atmosphere, and that the year-to-year periodicity is not wholly consistent with the timing of the Martian seasons. "A rigorous approach based on available evidence starts with the scientifically responsible default explanation that Mars is and always has been lifeless," Fries says. "Testing a hypothesis to the contrary requires a very strong body of evidence." Such tests could come soon, via data from the joint European and Russian ExoMars Trace Gas Orbiter. It arrived at Mars in 2016 and is now mapping concentrations of methane and other gases from on high.

For his part Webster says he has no preference among the different explanations, and believes it will take a long time before any final conclusions can be drawn. Such incremental progress is the whole point of NASA's Mars exploration program, Freissinet notes. "It's step by step," she says. "Mission after mission."

## About the Author

*Adam Mann is a journalist specializing in astronomy and physics. His work has appeared in* National Geographic, *the* Wall Street Journal, Wired, *and elsewhere.*

# Deep within Mars, Liquid Water Offers Hope for Life

## By Lee Billings

Located at the edge of a more than three-billion-year-old ice cap covering Mars's south pole, the region known as Planum Australe would rank high on any list of the Red Planet's least interesting locales. Frozen, flat and featureless, it seemingly offers little more than windblown dust and drifts of crystallized carbon dioxide for any aspiring explorer to see. Unless, that is, one could somehow peer deep underneath its frigid surface to the base of the ice cap some 1.5 kilometers below, where a lake of liquid water nearly three times larger than the island of Manhattan may lurk.

Discovered by a team of Italian scientists using three years' worth of data from the Mars Advanced Radar for Subsurface and Ionosphere Sounding (MARSIS) instrument on the European Space Agency's Mars Express orbiter, the potential lake is at least a few meters deep and might be a fixed, steady feature of the subsurface. If confirmed, this would be the first known reservoir of liquid water on present-day Mars—a keystone in the search for past or even present life on the Red Planet, potentially offering fresh clues about how Earth's neighbor so profoundly transformed billions of years ago from a warmer, wetter world to its current freeze-dried state. Announced July 25 at a press conference in Rome, the results are detailed in a study in the July 26 edition of Science. Although this is just one detection, the team wrote, "there is no reason to conclude that the presence of subsurface water on Mars is limited to a single location."

"The presence of a body of liquid water beneath Mars's south polar cap has various implications, opening new possibilities for the existence of microorganisms in the Martian environment," says Sebastian Lauro, a study co-author based at Roma Tre University in Rome. "Moreover, it provides a valuable confirmation that the water that once flowed abundantly over the Martian surface in the form of seas, lakes and rivers filled the voids in the subsurface."

For the past 12 years MARSIS has mapped the Martian underground using beams of low-frequency radar pulses, which can penetrate up to several kilometers below the surface. Although they pass relatively unscathed through most substances, these pulses reflect back up to the spacecraft each time they encounter boundaries between different materials, such as the interface of ice and bedrock. That reflection is particularly strong at interfaces with liquid water and shows up as a distinctively bright spot in visualizations of the data. Following up on preliminary detections of bright spots beneath Mars's southern ice cap dating back to 2007, the Italian team reprogrammed MARSIS to employ a more intensive scanning mode, then surveyed Planum Australe 29 times with the instrument between 2012 and 2015. Time and time again across the entire observing campaign the new MARSIS readings revealed a consistent 20-kilometer-wide bright spot nestled in a bowl-like depression beneath the ice cap in Planum Australe—a feature consistent with a sizable body of liquid water (or, to be fair, with water-saturated sediments more akin to subterranean sludge). The team then spent almost a year analyzing the data and another two years writing their paper and attempting to rule out nonaqueous explanations for what they had seen.

Billions of years ago Mars was a much more Earth-like place, where water pooled in seas, carved enormous canyons and bubbled from hot springs. Life, many astrobiologists speculate, may have had no difficulty getting started there. But early in its promising existence the planet somehow lost its way, transforming into a desiccated orb of dried-up oceans, rivers and lakes. Robotic missions to the planet's surface still find surprising echoes of that bygone time, such as patches of water-ice frost forming on rocks as well as water droplets condensing like dew on a lander's leg. Orbiters, too, have glimpsed what might be rivulets of water flowing down sun-bathed crater walls at the height of Martian summer. Perhaps life has also managed to endure in some diminished, limited way. But, if so, it would have to contend with a world in which all moisture quickly vanishes in the thin, cold air, leaving the surface dry as a bone. Still, the water that once flowed across the land had to go somewhere. Some of it was likely lost to space, due to Mars's diminutive gravitational field, but a significant fraction of the planet's aqueous inventory never really left, instead just freezing belowground. Now it appears not all of that buried watery wealth is frozen after all.

"The really exciting thing is that this is a stable body of liquid water that was observed in the radar data over three years, not just droplets that have been observed over a short period of time," says Anja Diez, a glaciologist at the Norwegian Polar Institute, who wrote an accompanying commentary about the discovery. The subsurface lake, Diez says, may be similar to those found via radar-sounding on Earth underneath ice sheets in Antarctica and Greenland.

Whether below an Earthly glacier or a Martian ice cap, the mechanism for melting is much the same: heat trickling up combines with the immense bulk of an insulating blanket of material pressing down to form lakes of meltwater. On Earth those lakes are often connected by channels, forming branching riverlike networks of water that extend across vast spaces below the ice. In the late 1980s Steve Clifford, a researcher now at the Planetary Science Institute, began exploring how similar hydrological activity could occur under both Mars's southern and northern polar caps and whether it might feed meltwater into worldwide aquifers he hypothesized should exist beneath the planet's permafrost. Clifford's models suggest huge amounts of liquid water could still be hidden in the planet's depths, providing a globe-spanning refuge for any life that retreated from the ever more inhospitable surface long ago.

"This finding is potentially of enormous significance," says Clifford, who was not involved with the study. "Based on analogy with Earth, if water still exists in the subsurface, there is no reason to believe that life which arose on Mars and evolved for underground conditions could not persist there into the present day.... If you do have liquid water as shallow as 1.5 kilometers beneath the surface [at Planum Australe], then liquid water is also likely to be present at greater depths here. And if you have conditions for life in one area of the planet that is in hydraulic continuity with other areas where liquid water also exists, you could have a very substantial subsurface biosphere that has survived since the planet's early history."

That life, however, would have to contend with another key factor making its aquatic environs possible: mineral salts that leach out of rocks and sediments to act as antifreeze. Suffusing the meltwater, the salts would create brines that remain liquid far below the typical freezing point of pure water. Such salts are known to exist in abundance in some Martian rocks and are the most likely cause of the dewlike droplets and crater-wall rivulets previously observed on the planet's surface. But Clifford holds out hope subsurface geothermal hotspots like those that power volcanoes and hot springs on Earth could sufficiently heat portions of the Martian underworld to allow liquid reservoirs to exist there without the need for life-sabotaging salt levels. Such a hot spot could, in fact, be responsible for the MARSIS team's newfound lake.

These conjectures must, for now, remain untested. The MARSIS instrument lacks sufficient sensitivity and resolution to clearly determine the thickness of this deposit or whether it is in fact connected to other similar bodies, although studies using more advanced radar instruments on an as yet unbuilt next generation of orbiters could clarify such details. For that matter, the detection itself is as yet uncorroborated: Another radar-sounding instrument called SHARAD (for "shallow radar") onboard NASA's Mars Reconnaissance Orbiter has also repeatedly scanned Planum Australe and other regions in search of buried water. But its beams cannot penetrate as deeply, and it has not replicated MARSIS's detection. Even so, according to Bruce Campbell, a SHARAD team member and senior scientist at the Smithsonian Institution, "it is possible that a targeted effort [by SHARAD] to collect data on more tracks across this region could build up enough echo strength to detect the reflector seen by MARSIS."

Ultimately "ground truth" may be required to solve the mystery of just how much water is locked away in Mars's underworld. But there are at present no public or private plans to build or launch missions, robotic or human, that would be capable of drilling or melting down to the depths probably required to directly sample meltwater anywhere on the planet—which, Clifford says, might be for the best.

"The possibility that life could currently exist somewhere beneath the polar ice reinforces the point that we must take care that our investigations do not needlessly contaminate Mars," he says. "That could not only make the result of any life-detection experiment ambiguous but could also contaminate a habitat that may be interconnected on a global basis, leading to a very serious impact on any native biosphere. I worry that unless we are very careful, we could end up responsible for the extinction of the very first life we ever detect on another planet."

## Referenced

Subsurface Radar Sounding of the South Polar Layered Deposits of Mars. Jeffrey J. Plaut in *Science*, Vol. 316, pages 92–95; April 6, 2007.

Mars Express Detects Water Buried under the South Pole of Mars. Press release from the European Space Agency, released July 25, 2018, 4:00 P.M. www.esa.int/spacein-images/Images/2018/07/

Radar Evidence of Subglacial Liquid Water on Mars. Roberto Orosei et al. in *Science*, Vol. 361, pages 490–493; August 3, 2018.

## About the Author

*Lee Billings is a senior editor for space and physics at* Scientific American.

# I'm Convinced We Found Evidence of Life on Mars in the 1970s

### By Gilbert V. Levin

We humans can now peer back into the virtual origin of our universe. We have learned much about the laws of nature that control its seemingly infinite celestial bodies, their evolution, motions and possible fate. Yet, equally remarkable, we have no generally accepted information as to whether other life exists beyond us, or whether we are, as was Samuel Coleridge's Ancient Mariner, "alone, alone, all, all alone, alone on a wide wide sea!" We have made only one exploration to solve that primal mystery. I was fortunate to have participated in that historic adventure as experimenter of the Labeled Release (LR) life detection experiment on NASA's spectacular Viking mission to Mars in 1976.

On July 30, 1976, the LR returned its initial results from Mars. Amazingly, they were positive. As the experiment progressed, a total of four positive results, supported by five varied controls, streamed down from the twin Viking spacecraft landed some 4,000 miles apart. The data curves signaled the detection of microbial respiration on the Red Planet. The curves from Mars were similar to those produced by LR tests of soils on Earth. It seemed we had answered that ultimate question.

When the Viking Molecular Analysis Experiment failed to detect organic matter, the essence of life, however, NASA concluded that the LR had found a substance mimicking life, but not life. Inexplicably, over the 43 years since Viking, none of NASA's subsequent Mars landers has carried a life detection instrument to follow up on these exciting results. Instead the agency launched a series of missions to Mars to determine whether there was ever a habitat suitable for life and, if so, eventually to bring samples to Earth for biological examination.

NASA maintains the search for alien life among its highest priorities. On February 13, 2019, NASA Administrator Jim Bridenstine said we might find microbial life on Mars. Our nation has now committed to sending astronauts to Mars. Any life there might threaten them, and us upon their return. Thus, the issue of life on Mars is now front and center.

Life on Mars seemed a long shot. On the other hand, it would take a near miracle for Mars to be sterile. NASA scientist Chris McKay once said that Mars and Earth have been "swapping spit" for billions of years, meaning that, when either planet is hit by comets or large meteorites, some ejecta shoot into space. A tiny fraction of this material eventually lands on the other planet, perhaps infecting it with microbiological hitch-hikers. That some Earth microbial species could survive the Martian environment has been demonstrated in many laboratories. There are even reports of the survival of microorganisms exposed to naked space outside the International Space Station (ISS).

NASA's reservation against a direct search for microorganisms ignores the simplicity of the task accomplished by Louis Pasteur in 1864. He allowed microbes to contaminate a hay-infusion broth, after which bubbles of their expired gas appeared. Prior to containing living microorganisms, no bubbles appeared. (Pasteur had earlier determinted that heating, or pasteurizing, such a substance would kill the microbes.) This elegantly simple test, updated to substitute modern microbial nutrients with the hay-infusion products in Pasteur's, is in daily use by health authorities around the world to examine potable water. Billions of people are thus protected against microbial pathogens.

This standard test, in essence, was the LR test on Mars, modified by the addition of several nutrients thought to broaden the prospects for success with alien organisms, and the tagging of the nutrients with radioactive carbon. These enhancements made the LR sensitive to the very low microbial populations postulated for Mars, should any be there, and reduced the time for detection of terrestrial microorganisms to about one hour. But on Mars, each

LR experiment continued for seven days. A heat control, similar to Pasteur's, was added to determine whether any response obtained was biological or chemical.

The Viking LR sought to detect and monitor ongoing metabolism, a very simple and fail-proof indicator of living microorganisms. Several thousand runs were made, both before and after Viking, with terrestrial soils and microbial cultures, both in the laboratory and in extreme natural environments. No false positive or false negative result was ever obtained. This strongly supports the reliability of the LR Mars data, even though their interpretation is debated.

In her recent book *To Mars with Love*, my LR co-experimenter Patricia Ann Straat provides much of the scientific detail of the Viking LR at lay level. Scientific papers published about the LR are available on my Web site.

In addition to the direct evidence for life on Mars obtained by the Viking LR, evidence supportive of, or consistent with, extant microbial life on Mars has been obtained by Viking, subsequent missions to Mars, and discoveries on Earth:

- Surface water sufficient to sustain microorganisms was found on Mars by Viking, Pathfinder, Phoenix and Curiosity;
- Ultraviolet (UV) activation of the Martian surface material did not, as initially proposed, cause the LR reaction: a sample taken from under a UV-shielding rock was as LR-active as surface samples;
- Complex organics, have been reported on Mars by Curiosity's scientists, possibly including kerogen, which could be of biological origin;
- Phoenix and Curiosity found evidence that the ancient Martian environment may have been habitable.
- The excess of carbon-13 over carbon-12 in the Martian atmosphere is indicative of biological activity, which prefers ingesting the latter;
- The Martian atmosphere is in disequilibrium: its $CO_2$ should long ago have been converted to CO by the sun's UV

light; thus the $CO_2$ is being regenerated, possibly by microorganisms as on Earth;

- Terrestrial microorganisms have survived in outer space outside the ISS;
- Ejecta containing viable microbes have likely been arriving on Mars from Earth;
- Methane has been measured in the Martian atmosphere; microbial methanogens could be the source;
- The rapid disappearance of methane from the Martian atmosphere requires a sink, possibly supplied by methanotrophs that could co-exist with methanogens on the Martian surface;
- Ghost-like moving lights, resembling will-O'-the-wisps on Earth that are formed by spontaneous ignition of methane, have been video-recorded on the Martian surface;
- Formaldehyde and ammonia, each possibly indicative of biology, are claimed to be in the Martian atmosphere;
- An independent complexity analysis of the positive LR signal identified it as biological;
- Six-channel spectral analyses by Viking's imaging system found terrestrial lichen and green patches on Mars rocks to have the identical color, saturation, hue and intensity;
- A wormlike feature was in an image taken by Curiosity;
- Large structures resembling terrestrial stromatolites (formed by microorganisms) were found by Curiosity; a statistical analysis of their complex features showed less than a 0.04 percent probability that the similarity was caused by chance alone;
- No factor inimical to life has been found on Mars.

In summary, we have: positive results from a widely-used microbiological test; supportive responses from strong and varied controls; duplication of the LR results at each of the two Viking sites; replication of the experiment at the two sites; and the failure over 43 years of any experiment or theory to provide a definitive nonbiological explanation of the Viking LR results.

What is the evidence against the possibility of life on Mars? The astonishing fact is that there is none. Furthermore, laboratory studies have shown that some terrestrial microorganisms could survive and grow on Mars.

NASA has already announced that its 2020 Mars lander will not contain a life-detection test. In keeping with well-established scientific protocol, I believe an effort should be made to put life detection experiments on the next Mars mission possible. I and my co-experimenter have formally and informally proposed that the LR experiment, amended with an ability to detect chiral metabolism, be sent to Mars to confirm the existence of life: non-biological chemical reactions do not distinguish between "left-handed" and "right-handed" organic molecules, but all living things do.

Moreover, the Chiral LR (CLR) could confirm and extend the Viking LR findings. It could determine whether any life detected were similar to ours, or whether there was a separate genesis. This would be a fundamental scientific discovery in its own right. A small, lightweight CLR has already been designed and its principle verified by tests. It could readily be turned into a flight instrument.

Meanwhile a panel of expert scientists should review all pertinent data of the Viking LR together with other and more recent evidence concerning life on Mars. Such an objective jury might conclude, as I did, that the Viking LR did find life. In any event, the study would likely produce important guidance for NASA's pursuit of its holy grail.

*The views expressed are those of the author(s) and are not necessarily those of Scientific American.*

## About the Author

*Gilbert V. Levin is an engineer and inventor; he was the principal investigator Labeled Release experiment on NASA Viking missions to Mars in the 1970s.*

# Until Recently, People Accepted the "Fact" of Aliens in the Solar System

By Caleb A. Scharf

O ne of the most intriguing aspects of the history of the human quest to discover whether or not there is other life in the universe, and whether any of it is recognizably intelligent in the way that we are, is just how much our philosophical mood has changed back and forth across the centuries.

Today we're witnessing a bit of a "golden age" in terms of active work towards answers. Much of that work stems from the overlapping revolutions in exoplanetary science and solar system exploration, and our ongoing revelations about the sheer diversity and tenacity of life here on Earth. Together these areas of study have given us places to look, phenomena to look for, and increased confidence that we're quick approaching the point where our technical prowess may cross the necessary threshold for finding some answers about life elsewhere.

Into that mix goes the search for extraterrestrial intelligence (SETI); as we've become more comfortable with the notion that the technological restructuring and repurposing of matter is something we can, and should, be actively looking for. If for no other reason than our own repurposing of matter, here on Earth, has become ever more vivid and fraught, and therefore critical to appreciate and modify in aid of long-term survival. But this search, labeled as both SETI and the quest for "technosignatures," still faces some daunting challenges—not least the catch-up required after decades of receiving a less-than-stellar allocation of scientific resources.

What is so fascinating is that in many respects we have already been here and done all of this before, just not recently, and not with the same set of tools that we now have to hand.

In western Europe, during the period from some four hundred years ago until last century, the question of life beyond the Earth seems to have been less of "if" and more of "what." Famous scientists like Christiaan Huygens wrote in his *Cosmotheoros* of *"So many Suns, so many Earths, and every one of them stock'd with so many Herbs, Trees and Animals...even the little Gentlemen round Jupiter and Saturn..."* And this sense of cosmic plurality wasn't uncommon. It was in almost all respects far simpler and more reasonable to assume that the wealth of life on Earth was simply repeated elsewhere. That is once one let go of a sense of earthly uniqueness.

In other words, in many quarters there was no "are we alone?" question being asked, instead the debate was already onto the details of how the life elsewhere in the cosmos went about its business.

In the 1700s and 1800s we had astronomers like William Herschel, or the more amateur Thomas Dick, not only proposing that our solar system, from the Moon to the outer planets, was overrun with lifeforms (Dick holding the record by suggesting that Saturn's rings held around 8 trillion individuals) but convincing themselves that they could see the evidence. Herschel, with his good telescopes, becoming convinced that there were forests on the Moon, in the Mare humorum, and speculating that the Sun's dark spots were actually holes in a glowing hot atmosphere, beneath which, a cool surface supported large alien beings.

Even though we might question some of their scientific standards, people like Herschel and Dick were indeed following the philosophy of life being everywhere, and elevating it to the level of any other observable phenomenon. Herschel was also applying the best scientific instruments he could at the time.

All the way into the 20th century, prior to the data obtained by the Mariner 4 flyby in 1965, the possibility that Mars had a more clement surface environment, and therefore life, still carried significant weight. Although there had been extreme claims like Percival Lowell's "canals" on Mars in the late 1800s and very early 1900s, astronomers of the time largely disagreed with these specific interpretations. Interestingly, that was because they simply couldn't reproduce the observations, finding the markings he associated with canals and civilizations to be largely non-existent (an example of how better data can discount pet theories). But aside from Lowell's distractions, the existence of a temperate climate of sorts on Mars was not easy to discount, nor was life on its surface. For example, Carl Sagan and Paul Swan published a paper just ahead of Mariner 4's arrival at Mars in which they wrote:

> *The present body of scientific evidence suggests, but does not unambiguously demonstrate, the existence of life on Mars. In particular, the photometrically observed waves of darkening which proceed from the vaporizing polar caps through the dark areas of the Martian surface have been interpreted in terms of seasonal biological activity.*

Suffice to say, this proposal went the way of many other overly optimistic ideas about finding life on the red planet. Although it is fascinating how well the periodic darkening phenomenon they discussed could indeed fit into a picture of a surface biosphere on Mars–and remains perhaps a rather sobering lesson in overinterpreting limited data.

But the key point is that we *have* actually more often than not been of a mindset that life is out there, and could explain certain cosmic observations. The problem has been that, as data has improved, and scrutiny has intensified, the presence of life has not revealed itself–from planetary exploration or from the search for extraterrestrial intelligence. And because of that we've swung to the other extreme, where the question has gone from "what" all the way back to "if."

Of course, we have also likely systematically underestimated the challenge across the centuries. Even today it is apparent that the search for structured radio emissions from technological life has thus far only scratched the surface of a complex parameter space; a fact beautifully quantified and articulated by Jason Wright and colleagues in 2018, as being much like looking in a hot tub of water to draw conclusions about the contents of Earth's oceans.

In that sense, perhaps the more fundamental question is whether or not we are, this time, technologically equipped to crack the puzzle once and for all. There is little doubt that our capacity to sense the most ethereal, fleeting phenomena in the cosmos is at an all time high. But there seems to be a fine line between acknowledging that exciting possibility and falling prey to the kind of hubris that some of our precursors fell prey to. Naturally, we say, *this* is the most special time in human existence, if we can only expand our minds and our efforts then all may be revealed!

Of course, none of us can know for sure which way this will all go. We might do better being very explicit about the uncertainty inherent in all of this, because it's actually incredibly exciting to have to face the unknown, and unknowable. What we shouldn't do is allow the unpredictable nature of this particular pendulum, swinging between possibilities, to dissuade us from trying.

## About the Author

*Caleb A. Scharf is director of astrobiology at Columbia University. He is author and co-author of more than 100 scientific research articles in astronomy and astrophysics. His work has been featured in publications such as* New Scientist, Scientific American, Science News, Cosmos Magazine, Physics Today *and* National Geographic. *For many years he wrote the* Life, Unbounded *blog for* Scientific American.

# Section 4: Geology on Mars

4.1   The Many Faces of Mars
      By Philip R. Christensen

4.2   Data Deluge: Texas Flood Canyon Offers Test of Hydrology
      Theories for Earth and Mars
      By John Matson

4.3   I Can Tell You about Mars
      By David Bressan

4.4   Martian Mile-High Mounds Mystery: The Answer Is
      Blowing in the Wind
      By Shannon Hall

4.5   Water on Mars May Be Trapped in the Planet's Crust,
      Not Lost to Space
      By Jonathan O'Callaghan

# The Many Faces of Mars

By Philip R. Christensen

Many people venture into the desert for its starkness and simplicity, but I go there for its complexity. The rocks of western Arizona, where I work, reveal one of the most tangled histories on Earth. Layers of carbonate limestones, silty mudstones, quartz sand and solidified lava show that within the past 600 million years, this area was a warm, shallow sea, then a muddy swamp, then a vast desert of shimmering hot dunes, then a glacial ice sheet, then a shallow sea once again. Erupting volcanoes formed islands like Japan, which in turn got shoved 100 miles onto the continent along massive faults, tilting the rock layers on edge and cooking them to create marble and quartzite. Uplift and erosion at last produced the desert landscape we see today.

This kind of detailed historical reconstruction has long been impossible for Mars. Within my lifetime, the Red Planet has been transformed from a point in the night sky into a land of towering volcanoes, dried-up riverbeds, ancient lakes and windswept lava plains. Clearly, Mars has one of the most glorious histories in the solar system. Yet scientists have been able to piece together only the sketchiest outlines of that history. For years, we have debated such sweeping questions as whether Mars was once "warm and wet" and Earth-like or "cold and dry" and barren like the moon, as though the story of an entire world could be reduced to a sound bite.

Over the past decade, though, we have entered the third great era of Mars exploration, the first two being the telescopic observations of the 19th century and the initial spacecraft reconnaissance of the 1960s and 1970s. Recent orbiter and rover missions have mapped the planet's topography, determined its mineralogy, imaged its surface in sufficient detail to interpret geologic processes, and merged orbital data with ground truth. Mars has finally become a place that I can study as a geologist does, using its rocks, minerals and landforms to weave a narrative.

What we have discovered is that Mars has experienced a striking diversity of processes and conditions throughout its history. The Mars we are coming to know has embraced environments ranging from bone-dry to soaking wet to blanketed with snow and ice. Simple labels no longer fit. Rather than "warm" or "cold," we ask: How warm? How wet? For how long? Where? The emerging answers bear on what compels so many of us to study the Red Planet: its potential for harboring life, either now or in the past.

## Two Places, Two Views

In January 2004 NASA landed two of the most complex machines ever built at two very different sites on Mars. Packed with cameras and spectrometers to determine soil and rock composition, the Spirit and Opportunity rovers set out to answer the central question of Martian geology: What has been the role of water? Spirit bounced down in Gusev Crater, which had been chosen for the shape of its landforms: images taken from orbit have long shown that a valley, Ma'adim, opens into the crater, as if Gusev was once a lake.

Initially the site proved to be somewhat of a letdown. Spirit found no signs of past water. What it saw were volcanic rocks, which spectrometers indicated were composed of olivine and pyroxene, minerals broken down by even the barest amount of liquid water. The rocks could not have been exposed to any significant amount of water in the three billion years or so since erupting. As Spirit climbed into the Columbia Hills, which overlook the landing site, the situation got more interesting. There the rover discovered high abundances of sulfur salts. Evidently, volcanic rocks had been ground into small grains and then cemented together by salt, a process that may have involved liquid water percolating through the rocks or sulfuric acid reacting with minerals that were already in the rock. Despite this hint of water, however, these rocks still contained significant amounts of olivine and pyroxene. Thus, even on what may once have been a lake bed, water appears to have played a minor role over the past few billion years.

# Overview/Martian Oddities

The Spirit and Opportunity rovers have been rambling around Mars for one and a half years, while three orbiters have mapped the planet's topography and mineral composition with a precision once available only for Earth.

Until these missions, the primary evidence for past water on Mars was morphological: landform shapes, which are suggestive but ambiguous. Now the main evidence is mineralogical (the presence of iron oxides and sulfate salts) and textural (spherules and ripples in bedrock), leaving no doubt that the Opportunity landing site, at least, is an ancient lake bed.

Yet the geologic history of the planet varies tremendously, and bizarrely, with location and time. Much of the planet has seen scarcely a drop of water; even the Opportunity site went through long dry spells. Other geologic features, such as volcanoes, are also unexpectedly diverse.

The Opportunity rover headed to the plains of Meridiani. The selection of this site marked a new phase in humanity's exploration of the solar system: never before had planetary scientists sent a probe to a location for its mineralogy. Early spacecraft missions to Mars ascertained the composition of the surface in terms of chemical elements, but identifying the minerals—the compounds and crystal structures that these elements formed—required the Thermal Emission Spectrometer (TES), an instrument I developed for NASA's Mars Global Surveyor orbiter, which reached the planet in 1997. In the mineral maps we prepared, Meridiani stood out for its high abundance of crystalline hematite.

This iron oxide, common on Earth, forms by several processes, most of which involve water. One is the precipitation from fluids circulating through sediments; another, the deposition and dehydration of water-bearing iron minerals such as goethite, a reddish-brown mineral found in many desert soils. The Meridiani hematite-rich rocks appeared to be finely layered and easily eroded; they sat on top of the older, heavily cratered surface, suggesting a sedimentary deposit; and they filled in preexisting channels and other low areas of topography, suggesting that these rocks were deposited in water rather than draped across the landscape as volcanic ash or windblown dust.

Within days of landing, Opportunity confirmed that Meridiani had once been underwater. It immediately spotted outcrops of layered sedimentary rocks, the first ever seen on Mars. The rocks were so full of sulfate—30 to 40 percent by weight—that only the evaporation of sulfur-rich water could account for them. The sulfates at Gusev were not nearly so extensive. The hematite took the form of spheres (dubbed "blueberries") one to five millimeters across that were embedded in the rock layers and scattered all over the ground.

The largest outcrop that Opportunity explored, named Burns Cliff, appeared to be a series of preserved sand dunes that were wetted by surface and ground waters. Many of the grains in them were sulfates formed from the evaporation of standing water, perhaps in the level areas (known as playas) between the dunes. Judging from analogous features on Earth, the rocks of Burns Cliff took thousands to hundreds of thousands of years to form. The spherical hematite grains may have been created later from iron-rich fluids circulating through sediments. For the first time ever on Mars, scientists investigated an outcrop in the multifaceted way geologists on Earth do.

Even the morphology of the Meridiani plains, one of the flattest landscapes observed on any planet, looks like a lake bed. The extent of hematite mapped from orbit suggests it was an isolated large lake or small sea rather than part of a global ocean. Several craters to the south and west of the main hematite deposit also have hematite-rich layered rocks; perhaps they were separate lakes.

In short, it was as if the two rovers had landed on two completely different planets: one drier than any desert on Earth, the other a land of a thousand lakes. Are these the only possibilities, or is Martian geology even more varied? Do these two sites, thousands of kilometers apart, represent the total range of rock compositions and aqueous activity on Mars? To answer these broad questions, scientists have looked anew at data taken from orbit.

## Lava Land

Over the past eight years, the TES instrument has discovered that Martian rocks and sands are composed almost entirely of the volcanic minerals feldspar, pyroxene and olivine—the components of basalt. In the spring of 2004 the European Space Agency's Mars Express orbiter, carrying the OMEGA near-infrared spectrometer, joined the effort and verified the extensive presence of these minerals. Olivine is exposed more than 4.5 kilometers below the surface in the walls of the Valles Marineris canyon system; it appears all over the equatorial plains, including the floors of channels. The discovery of basalt did not come as a great surprise. Basalt also covers much of Earth and the moon; the lava that oozes across Hawaii is basalt. It is a pristine type of lava—formed from the first stage of melting of the planet's mantle—and on Earth it continuously erupts from mid-ocean ridges to create the seafloor.

Another discovery, though, was unexpected. Whereas the rocks in the ancient heavily cratered terrains were basaltic, the younger rocks of the northern lowlands resembled a more highly evolved type of lava called andesite: they contained more glass, more silica-rich minerals and fewer iron-bearing minerals. On Earth, andesites typically form when descending tectonic plates mix water into subterranean molten rock. The possible existence of andesites on Mars is intriguing. It may indicate that the Martian mantle is wetter than Earth's or that younger lavas melted at different temperatures or pressures than the older basalts. To be sure, some scientists propose that the supposed andesites are basalts masquerading as such; a fog of water or acid could react with the minerals to create an andesitelike veneer. Researchers may have to wait for detailed surface studies of these rocks to resolve this question.

The TES instrument has fairly low spatial resolution: a pixel is several kilometers across. So the true variety of Martian mineralogy started to become apparent only in 2001, when THEMIS, an infrared camera that my group developed for another NASA orbiter, Mars Odyssey, began mapping the planet with 100-meter resolution. It and OMEGA have revealed a diversity of igneous rock compositions that rivals Earth's.

Near the Martian equator sits a volcano 1,100 kilometers in diameter named Syrtis Major. A series of collapsed craters, or calderas, lie at its summit. The bulk of the volcano is basaltic, but the slopes are dotted with cones and lava flows consisting of glassy, silica-rich lavas called dacites. This rock type originates in the magma chambers that underlie volcanoes. As magma cools, the first minerals to crystallize are olivine and pyroxene, which are rich in iron and magnesium. They settle to the bottom of the chamber, leaving the remaining magma enriched in silica and aluminum—from which dacites emerge. The central peaks of several craters on the flanks of Syrtis Major are made up of an even more silica-rich rock, granite, that may have formed by extreme crystal separation or by large-scale remelting of earlier basalts.

Researchers conclude that this volcano went through many stages of development. Basaltic lava first erupted from the center and built up the volcano. As the magma evolved chemically, it withdrew from the chamber underneath the summit, causing the ground there to collapse and feeding eruptions on the flanks. Not only are Martian volcanoes huge, they are surprisingly complex.

## And There Will Come Soft Rains

Just as important as what Mars has is what it lacks. Quartz is common on Earth but exceedingly rare on Mars, indicating that granite, from which it forms, is scarce. Nor is there evidence for metamorphic minerals such as slate or marble, produced when volcanic or sedimentary rocks are subjected to high pressure or temperature. The main implication is that Mars does not have tectonics capable of driving rocks to great depths (where they are heated and squeezed) and then bringing them back to the surface.

Earth has vast deposits of carbonate rocks such as limestone, which precipitated from warm, carbon dioxide–rich oceans. Planetary scientists, reasoning that Mars used to be warmer and wetter, thought it, too, would have thick layers of carbonates. But none have been found. That means any oceans were cold or short-lived or ice-covered or otherwise hostile to carbonates. The ubiquitous dust does contain small amounts of carbonate, but it probably formed by direct interaction with water vapor in the atmosphere rather than liquid water on the surface. Another class of water-related minerals, clays, is also rare on Mars—again suggesting that the planet has been mostly dry. That accords with the widespread presence of the water-shy minerals olivine and pyroxene.

In this sense, what Spirit saw at Gusev is more representative of Mars than what Opportunity found at Meridiani. And yet Meridiani is not the only place where lakes appear in the orbital images. Aram Chaos, a 280-kilometer-diameter crater, has an outflow channel and is filled with layered rocks that contain hematite. Gigantic blocks of rock litter the crater floor. It looks as though a torrent of subsurface water was catastrophically released, causing the overlying terrain to collapse. Some of the water ponded in the crater, forming the layers of hematite-bearing sediments.

Similarly, troughs in Valles Marineris contain hematite-bearing rocks in fine, easily eroded layers, matching what one expects from deposition in standing water. These rocks, and others throughout the equatorial region, are rich in sulfates, a telltale sign of water-lain sediments. The lakes may have undergone numerous episodes of inundation, evaporation (and possibly freezing), and desiccation. In addition to the ancient lake beds are regions carved with dense networks of channels, seemingly created by rainfall and surface runoff. Some researchers have argued that Mars had extensive oceans: images and topographic data hint at shorelines and smooth ocean floors.

Together these discoveries provide strong evidence that water was stable in isolated regions for brief periods. What factors caused water to accumulate and remain stable at these sites? A leading guess is a combination of geothermal heat, large doses of salt (which lowered the freezing temperature) and a protective covering of ice. Large meteor impacts may have occasionally thickened and warmed the atmosphere.

But the idea of a once Earth-like planet seems to be passé. The overwhelming impression from the global mineral mapping is of an ancient surface whose original volcanic minerals are still preserved, little altered by water. Even at Meridiani, basaltic sands lie atop the lake sediments, indicating that the site has been parched for two billion to three billion years. Lakes and riverlike networks do exist, but water may have flowed through them only briefly. It is possible that water remained frozen for most of the time, was occasionally released and quickly refroze. Still, planetary scientists puzzle over how a world that was so arid in general could have been so watery at certain places and times.

## Planet of the Long Seasons

Mars's epic past tends to get the most attention, but two developments have reinvigorated study of its present-day activity. First is the growing consensus that Mars has been geologically active in the recent past. Most large volcanoes and lava plains are old, dating to the first half of the planet's history, but the lack of meteor impact craters on lava flows in regions such as Athabasca suggests they are young (by a geologist's standards), the result of eruptions within the past few million years. Researchers have looked for active volcanic or geothermal hot spots in nighttime infrared images but so far have seen none. Mars appears to have cooled to the point where volcanism is very rare, although lava does occasionally erupt onto the surface.

The second is the discovery that Mars has colossal reservoirs of frozen water that migrate around the planet as its climate changes. To begin with, both poles have deposits of ice or ice-rich sediments that are up to several kilometers thick over a combined area nearly twice the size of Arizona. Infrared temperature readings in the 1970s demonstrated that the north polar cap is water ice but did not settle the composition of the south polar cap. Its surface temperature matches that of carbon dioxide ice, but might water ice lie underneath? Recent temperature readings by THEMIS have detected water ice poking through in certain places, so the answer seems to be yes.

Adding to the known inventory of water is the underground ice detected by the Gamma Ray Spectrometer and the High Energy Neutron Detector instruments on Mars Odyssey. These instruments measure gamma rays and neutrons, which are produced when cosmic rays collide with atoms in the soil. The energy distribution of gamma photons and neutrons reveals the elemental composition of the soil to a depth of several meters. For instance, hydrogen strongly absorbs neutrons, so a dearth of neutrons implies subsurface hydrogen—most probably the $H_2$ of $H_2O$. In the regions between 60 degrees latitude and each pole, water appears to make up more than 50 percent of the soil. Ice abundances this high could not have formed by the simple diffusion of water vapor from the atmosphere into the pores of the soil. Instead the ice must have been deposited as snow or frost.

Unusual landforms seen throughout the midlatitudes also hint at ice. A basketball-textured terrain occurs between 30 and 50 degrees latitude in both hemispheres; it may form as soil warms up and ice evaporates, causing the soil to crumble apart. A second type of deposit, found in hollows on cold, pole-facing slopes, is a layer of material up to 10 meters thick—a possible remnant of nearly pure water snow. One of the most remarkable discoveries has been the small, fresh gullies at midlatitudes, perhaps the result of spring water, melting of near-surface ice, or melting of snowpacks from the bottom up.

All these water-related features suggest that Mars, like Earth, goes through a cycle of ice ages. The tilt of the planet's spin axis oscillates by as much as 20 degrees over a period of 125,000 years. When the tilt is modest, the poles are the coldest places on the planet. More snow falls there than evaporates, leading to a net accumulation of ice. As the tilt increases, the poles receive more sunlight and warm up, at the expense of the midlatitudes. Water tends to move from the poles toward the equator. As snow builds up on the surface, running water can trickle out. Today the midlatitudes are warming up, and the snow cover has mostly disappeared. If the ice-age model is correct, they will return over the next 25,000 to 50,000 years.

The story of Mars science is like the tale of the blind men describing an elephant: the geology seems to change depending on where you look. The planet is a richly textured place with an amazingly dynamic present and an intricate, even paradoxical, past. Its volcanic rocks are as diverse as Earth's, and the manifestations of water vary tremendously. The planet experienced heavy flooding and perhaps even rainfall earlier in its history, yet its ancient rocks still contain minerals that quickly break down in a wet environment. The climate is dry and cold, yet the Opportunity rover found itself on the floor of an ancient sea, indicating that the climate used to be very different. Liquid water is unstable under present conditions, yet gullies formed recently and may continue to do so.

The diversity of surface environments from place to place and time to time is one of the most hopeful indicators for Martian biology: it provides a rich suite of environments where life may have taken hold. Water was abundant in lakes for long, if intermittent, periods. It may have been around long enough for inanimate matter to come alive. Organisms may still cling to life, hibernating during the cold spells and thawing out when climate conditions improve. The remnant snow patches, gullies and similar regions would be an excellent place to search for life on future robotic missions.

## For Further Reading

Global Mapping of Martian Hematite Mineral Deposits: Remnants of Water-Driven Processes on Early Mars. P. R. Christensen, R. V. Morris, M. D. Lane, J. L. Bandfi eld and M. C. Malin in *Journal of Geophysical Research*, Vol. 106, Part 10, pages 23,873–23,885; 2001.

Morphology and Composition of the Surface of Mars: Mars Odyssey THEMIS Results. Philip R. Christensen et al. in *Science*, Vol. 300, No. 5628, pages 2056–2061; June 27, 2003.

Spirit at Gusev Crater. Special issue of *Science*, Vol. 305, No. 5685, pages 793–845; August 6, 2004.

Opportunity at Meridiani Planum. Special issue of *Science*, Vol. 306, No. 5702, pages 1697–1756; December 3, 2004.

*Roving Mars: Spirit, Opportunity, and the Exploration of the Red Planet*. Steve
Squyres. Hyperion, 2005.

## About the Author

*Philip R. Christensen got interested in geology as a kid traveling throughout the American West. He first looked at Mars through a telescope his parents gave him when he was 12. Now a professor at Arizona State University at Tempe, he is the world's leading expert on the composition of the Martian surface. His research team developed the infrared instruments for the Mars Global Surveyor, Mars Odyssey and Mars Exploration Rover missions. In 2003 NASA awarded him its Exceptional Scientific Achievement Medal for his pioneering scientific observations of Mars in the infrared. Since the mid-1990s he has also used spacecraft observations to study environmental and urban development problems on Earth.*

# Data Deluge: Texas Flood Canyon Offers Test of Hydrology Theories for Earth and Mars

By John Matson

A geologic scar left by a catastrophic Texas flood in 2002 is providing an unexpected scientific benefit. A new study demonstrates how researchers can use a channel carved by floodwaters pouring over the dam of a flooded reservoir as a laboratory to test scientific theories of how such canyons are formed. The research could help to inform the hydrological histories of Earth and Mars by indicating the kind of imprints large, sudden floods leave on a planet's surface.

The storm that struck central Texas eight years ago wreaked havoc on the region, which President George W. Bush declared a disaster area. Floodwaters killed 12 people and damaged 48,000 homes in dozens of counties, according to a report from the U.S. Geological Survey (USGS). At Canyon Lake, a reservoir north of San Antonio, water rushed over the dam's spillway, pouring into the valley below. Within days a 50-meter-wide channel now known as the Canyon Lake Gorge had been carved into the soil and bedrock, drastically transforming the landscape on a short timescale.

Thanks to the recent nature of the event, along with USGS monitoring, extensive topographic information and eyewitness reports, researchers can explore the geologic aftermath of a large flood whose discharge and duration are well constrained. That is a rare if not unprecedented opportunity, says California Institute of Technology geologist Michael Lamb, a co-author of the study published online June 20 by *Nature Geoscience* describing the gorge's formation. (*Scientific American* is part of Nature Publishing Group.)

He became interested in the gorge while studying canyon formation on Earth and Mars during a 2008–2009 postdoctoral fellowship at the University of Texas at Austin, about 100 kilometers away. Along with his colleague Mark Fonstad, a geographer at

Texas State University–San Marcos, Lamb found that the landscape below Canyon Lake had been remodeled in just three days or so, during which hundreds of thousands of cubic meters of rock and sediment were flushed downstream.

Mars's surface is dotted with deltas, floodplains and gullies that indicate a rich hydrological history for the Red Planet, even though conditions today preclude the appearance of liquid water there. Some researchers believe that conditions were once much different and that Mars could have once had vast oceans of standing water, which would bode well for the past development of life on the planet, but others have come to believe that the water activity was confined to short-lived bursts of rainfall or catastrophic flooding.

Most large floods on Earth, Lamb notes, occur in rivers or other areas where water has been carving its way through the land over long timescales. The uniqueness of the Texas site is that the valley below the dam had historically been essentially dry land, making the changes attributable to the 2002 flood plainly visible. Victor Baker, a hydrologist, planetary scientist and geologist at the University of Arizona in Tucson, says that even with the ubiquity of sensing and imaging data, and despite the heavy rains endemic to Texas, it may be a while before researchers are able to observe the fresh carving of another brand-new channel.

With the amount of flood information available, Lamb says, Canyon Lake Gorge can provide a field experiment to test theories of how water flows form channels and canyons. That would come in handy for a place like Mars, where ancient channels are all that remain; planetary scientists must infer the Red Planet's hydrologic history from the way water shaped the surface. "It's important to reaffirm these reconstructions to understand the geologic history of Earth as well as Mars," Lamb says.

The 2002 Texas flood was powerful, plucking meter-size limestone boulders out of the bedrock and carrying them away to leave a channel that in places exceeds 12 meters in depth. It still does not hold a candle to the ancient megafloods that shaped Earth and Mars, Baker notes, but it is closer than most lab research comes to replicating those conditions. "An experiment like this one, which is intermediate between what we can do in a lab and what's on Mars, is relevant because it shows us how these physical principles interact to create outcomes that we can see," he says.

## About the Author

*John Matson is a former reporter and editor for* Scientific American *who has written extensively about astronomy and physics.*

# I Can Tell You about Mars

## By David Bressan

In 1849 the Italian chemist J. Usiglio performed a set of evaporation experiments with seawater along the French Riviera and established the order in which evaporite minerals precipitate from an aqueous environment. On earth these minerals are mostly gypsum and halite, associated with borates, potassium and magnesium salts. These minerals (not surprisingly) if found in a stratigraphic column are compelling evidence for the former presence of water.

Already from the orbit the Mars Global Surveyor identified terrains on Mars composed of a stratified material, covering a more rugged and cratered relief. The interpretation for this terrain ranged from volcanic lava sheets to aeolian sediment to deposits formed in water. To clarify the origin of these layers a field-investigation was necessary. In 2004 the Opportunity rover landed in the Eagle Crater located on the Meridiani Planum—a flat, uniform plain with few impact craters and delimitated by cliffs with recognizable stratified structure. Opportunity spotted some outcrops in the small crater, however the exposed stratigraphic column was very short. The rover was therefore directed to the larger Endurance Crater (with a diameter of 200 m).

The outer rim of this crater provided an unique outcrop—soon named Burns Cliff, after Roger Burns, who predicted the mineralogy of the Martian rocks (composed mainly of ultrabasic minerals, like Olivine, and ferric sulfate minerals) based on the preliminary results obtained by the Viking missions.

Along the slope of the cliff geologists recognized a succession of rock types, or facies, named informally Burns Formation, the only extraterrestrial geologic formation at the time. The Burns Formation consists almost entirely of sandstone with grains of basalt, oxides, silicates and evaporite minerals (calcium and magnesium- sulfates, chlorides and phosphates).

The Burns Formation can be subdivided in three members:

121

- A lower unit of cross-bedded sandstone, probably sand dunes formed on a dry lakebed
- A middle unit with finely laminated sandstone, interpreted as ancient sand sheet deposits, overlies the lower unit with an Rare cross-laminated layers maybe represents sporadic flood events. This units displays various effects of groundwater infiltration, like dissolution of minerals and precipitation of new ones. Convoluted layers formed probably when minerals expanded due chemical reactions with the groundwater.
- The upper unit consists of finely laminated sandstone, however layers of cross-laminated sandstone are more frequent. These layers show also a particular sedimentary feature named "festoon cross-bedding"—concave, intersecting sets of thin layers, found on earth only in cross-sections of subaqueous ripples.

The Burns Formation records the transition from a dry dune-field to a wet "playa" environment. The infiltrated water stabilized the grains against erosion by Martian wind and flat sheets of sandstone formed. Sporadic flood events formed ripples, during dry phases evaporite minerals precipitated from the evaporating water. In later times Meridiani-Planum was covered for longer periods with water—maybe a shallow lake formed. This transition from dry to wet conditions occurred probably many times in Mars' past , as the dunes of the lower unit are already formed by reworked evaporite minerals from older playa sediments.

The age of Burns Formation is unknown. The lack of big impact craters and the few small craters suggest a relatively "young" age of Noachian (4.1- 3.7 billion years) to Lower Hesperian (3.7-3.0 billion years).

The landing site of Curiosity was selected for similar criteria as the Opportunity site. Gale Crater is a 3.7 billion year old Ghost crater, once covered by layers of sediments, erosion later exhumated the crater. Aeolis Mons, the central elevation inside the crater, is a mesa with stratified structure—the first picture send to earth seems promising...

*The views expressed are those of the author(s) and are not necessarily those of Scientific American.*

## For Further Reading

CARR,M. H. (2006): *The Surface of Mars.* Cambridge Planetary Science Series—Cambridge University Press—New York: 307

GROTZINGER, J.P., ARVIDSON, R.E., BELL III, J.F.; CALVIN, W.; CLARK, B.C.; FIKE, D.A.; GOLOMBEK, M.; GREELEY, R.; HALDEMANN, A.; HERKENHOFF, K.E.; JOLLIFF, B.L.; KNOLL, A.H.; MALIN, M.; McLENNAN, S.M.; PARKER, T.; SODERBLOM, L.; SOHL-DICKSTEIN, J.N.; SQUYRES, S.W.; TOSCA, N.J. & WATTERS, W.A. (2005): Stratigraphy and sedimentology of a dry to wet eolian depositional system, Burns formation, Meridiani Planum, Mars. *Earth and Planetary Science Letters* 240: 11-72

## About the Author

*My name is David Bressan and I'm a freelance geologist working mainly in the Austroalpine crystalline rocks and the South Alpine Palaeozoic and Mesozoic cover-sediments in the Eastern Alps. I graduated with a project on Rock Glaciers dynamics and hydrology, this phase left a special interest for quaternary deposits and modern glacial environments. During my research on glaciers, studying old maps, photography and reports on the former extent of these features, I became interested in history, especially the development of geomorphologic and geological concepts by naturalists and geologists. Living in one of the key areas for the history of geology, I combine field trips with the historic research done in these regions, accompanied by historic maps and depictions. I discuss broadly also general geological concepts, especially in glaciology, seismology, volcanology, palaeontology and the relationship of society and geology.*

# Martian Mile-High Mounds Mystery: The Answer Is Blowing in the Wind

By Shannon Hall

Rising from the floor of Gale Crater on Mars, a stack of sedimentary rock called Mount Sharp towers 5.5 kilometers above the ground. The mountain is only a little shorter than North America's tallest peak, Alaska's Mount Denali (nearly 6.2 kilometers high). Monstrous mountains on Earth are usually created by colliding plates of the planet's outer shell or by erupting volcanoes. But Mars does not have this kind of plate activity and its volcanoes have probably not been active for at least 500 million years. So planetary scientists have been stumped as to how Mount Sharp—and dozens of other giant peaks that rise from various Martian craters—formed. It has been an enduring puzzle since NASA's Viking spacecraft first spotted these mounds in the 1970s.

Now research lends support to the idea that winds in Mars's thin atmosphere, which can gust up to 95 kilometers per hour, built Mount Sharp over billions of years by carving away surrounding rock that once filled the crater to the brim, like an artist scraping a sculpture from a block of stone. The findings were published on March 31 in the journal *Geophysical Research Letters*.

Mackenzie Day, a geology graduate student at The University of Texas at Austin and her colleagues attacked this mystery using an old elementary school science project method: They built a miniature crater. Theirs was precise, 30 centimeters wide and four centimeters deep, and loaded with damp sand to represent the sediments that likely once filled the crater. The scientists then placed their small facsimile in a wind tunnel and turned on the fan. The wind first formed a crescent-shaped gash in the damp sand, its ends pointing away from the fan. That gash then widened until it became a ringlike moat, leaving the sand in the center intact. Over time the moat deepened until it reached the crater's floor, but the high pile of sand

in the middle remained—an indication that wind erosion can form
what scientists saw on Mars. "That was clear enough," says Gary
Kocurek, Day's advisor and a geologist at U.T. Austin. "But it's one
thing to have a simple little model in a wind tunnel. We wanted to
get a better quantification." So Day, Kocurek and their colleagues
then built a computer model to better picture how airflow interacts
with the crater's rim in a Martian environment.

Ralph Milliken, a geologist at Brown University who was not
involved in the study, is impressed by the way the team integrated
physical models with numerical simulations. "It's pretty rare to see
that sort of thing in the planetary science world," he says. Although
the models cannot disprove another wind-driven theory—that breezes
built these mounds up by carrying rock grains to them, rather than
carving them out—they do nicely explain certain features that the
other theory has yet to account for. For instance, Kristen Bennett,
a geology graduate student at Arizona State University in Tempe
has found that many Martian mounds are off-center within their
craters. "This [model] shows that wind erosion can do that," she
says. Once the central mound has been dug out, the pelting wind
will push it toward one side of the crater.

On Earth these gradual effects are often obscured by faster-
moving forces, like plate tectonics and volcanism. "Wind is powerful
but it's slow," Day says. "On Mars these craters have been exposed
to the surface for three billion years so there's a lot of time to do
that work and to get that material out of there in a way that we've
never really seen on Earth. So it's a result that speaks to the power
of wind in a way that we've never really seen before."

The mounds also provide an excellent view of Mars' evolution
from a wet habitable world to the dry inhospitable one we see
today. The layers of Mount Sharp shift from rocky strata at the
bottom, laid down in wet times, to other layers at the top, put
down in dry periods. Although a change from a water-driven
world to a wind-driven world can be seen in specific places on
Earth (the iconic sand dunes of the Sahara Desert, for example,
are river deposits reworked by the wind), it occurred globally

on Mars. "So that's what we see in these mounds—it's the whole scenario captured," Kocurek says. In one spot, scientists can study the transformation of an entire planet.

## About the Author

*Shannon Hall is an award-winning freelance science journalist based in the Rocky Mountains. She specializes in writing about astronomy, geology and the environment.*

# Water on Mars May Be Trapped in the Planet's Crust, Not Lost to Space

By Jonathan O'Callaghan

Mars had water—until it didn't. Scientists thinks that about four billion years ago, the planet had substantial amounts of liquid water on its surface, enough to form rivers, lakes, seas, and even oceans—and perhaps also to support life. But something happened in the following billion years, triggering the loss of this water from the surface until all that was left was the cold, dry wasteland of a world that we see today. Why and how that happened remains somewhat of a mystery. "We don't exactly know why the water levels decreased and Mars became arid," says Eva Scheller of the California Institute of Technology.

In recent years, results from NASA's Mars-orbiting MAVEN spacecraft suggested the driver of this water depletion may have been atmospheric loss. Long ago, for reasons unknown, Mars lost its strong magnetic field, exposing the planet to atmosphere-eroding outbursts from the sun. As a result, much of Mars's air escaped to space, presumably carrying away most of the planet's water with it. But in a new paper published this week in the journal *Science*, Scheller and her colleagues argue this process alone cannot explain Mars's modern-day aridity. Instead they say that a substantial amount of the planet's water—between 30 and 99 percent—retreated into the crust, where it remains today, in a process known as crustal hydration.

"That loss [to space] would have to be very large to explain the loss of all of Mars's water," said Bethany Ehlmann of Caltech, a co-author on the study, in a press briefing at this week's virtually hosted Lunar and Planetary Science Conference, where the research was presented. "We realized we needed to pay attention to the evidence from the last 10 to 15 years of Mars exploration in terms of the nature of water in the Martian crust."

Using this swathe of evidence from a variety of Mars missions, the team found that the rate of atmospheric loss today was not enough to explain the disappearance of all Mars's water.

Additionally, the observed ratio of deuterium to hydrogen in the Martian atmosphere—an important clue in working out its watery past—was also not consistent with all of the planet's water being lost to space. Whereas hydrogen is light enough to easily slip away from a planet's gravitational grip, the element's heavier isotope deuterium cannot. Thus, a relative dearth of deuterium in the atmosphere today suggests that less water may have been lost in this way than was thought. An alternative explanation was needed.

Crustal hydration—in which water is incorporated into the crystalline structure of minerals—is a natural choice for that explanation. And in fact, it was previously proposed as an important mechanism for Martian water loss. Various lines of evidence convincingly show that the process must have occurred at certain points in the planet's history. For example, results from a neutron spectrometer instrument on NASA's Mars Odyssey spacecraft, which arrived at the planet in 2001, showed that, "basically everywhere, the crust had at least 2 percent water," Ehlmann says. "In the equator, that's water in soils and rocks." Later findings from NASA's Mars Reconnaissance Orbiter corroborated those results, mapping hydrated minerals on the surface of Mars. "It became very clear that it was common, and not rare, to find evidence of water alteration," she adds.

This crustal-hydration scenario would not mean Mars hides a liquid-water wonderland in its subsurface. Rather, because the water would be locked in minerals, the Martian crust could be especially enriched in clays and hydrated salts. The fact that, on Earth, this process has not robbed us of our oceans may be linked to plate tectonics, which allow the rock-locked water to be efficiently released through volcanic activity. On a planet free of plate tectonics such as Mars, however, this water would remain trapped.

If Mars's current rate of atmospheric loss is the same as it was long ago, then the figure of crustal hydration is likely closer to the 99 percent estimate, Scheller says. "But where we get uncertainty

is what the atmospheric structure of Mars was like [in the past],"
she says. "There are different elements that can make that loss
rate to space become quite high." One possible way is Martian
dust storms, which can dramatically increase the loss rates, says
Paul Mahaffy, director of the Solar System Exploration Division at
NASA's Goddard Space Flight Center and a principal investigator
on instruments on the Curiosity rover on the surface of Mars
and on MAVEN. During a global dust storm, he says, "a year's
worth of hydrogen from water could be lost in just 45 days. So
the history of water loss over time [on Mars] is complex and not
full constrained."

No matter how high the loss rate was, however, a "significant
amount of water would have been going into the crust," Scheller
says—likely more than half the planet's total. The team estimates
that Mars would have lost between 40 and 95 percent of its water
via this process in the planet's Noachian period, which stretches
from 4.1 billion to 3.7 billion years ago. But even later in Mars's
history, bursts of volcanic activity could have recycled some of the
subsurface moisture, potentially giving the planet's habitability
a much-needed boost. "You may have episodic habitability," says
Michael Meyer, lead scientist of NASA's Mars Exploration Program at
NASA headquarters in Washington, D.C. "The real question is what
these [volcanic] rates were. We think water was available 3.5 billion
years ago. What about three billion years ago?"

Understanding how and when Mars lost its water is therefore
crucial to knowing if life could have existed there—and for how
long. "The persistence of surface water could be highly relevant
to the possible emergence and existence of life on Mars," Mahaffy
says. Current and future missions could help us better answer the
question. One such effort is the International Mars Ice Mapper
mission, a collaboration among NASA, Japan, Canada and Italy
with a proposed launch later this decade. "Although it's designed
to look for water itself, it can give you [subsurface] layers," Meyer
says. "And if you're able to identify what the layers are, you can do
some volume calculations."

Meanwhile NASA's Perseverance rover, which landed on Mars last month, could also provide useful results on how extensive hydrated minerals are at its landing site, Jezero Crater. More importantly, it will collect samples that could help delve into this problem further once they are brought back to Earth next decade. "We can measure the deuterium-to-hydrogen ratio in the water in those," Meyer says. "That will help us sort out what ancient parts of Mars [were like]."

## About the Author

*Jonathan O'Callaghan is a freelance journalist covering commercial spaceflight, space exploration and astrophysics. Follow him on Twitter @Astro_Jonny.*

# Section 5: The Dynamic Martian Climate

5.1   Global Climatic Change on Mars
      By Jeffrey S. Kargel and Robert G. Strom

5.2   The Distant Shores of Mars
      By Caleb A. Scharf

5.3   Dust Bowl Mars
      By Caleb A. Scharf

5.4   NASA'S Curiosity Rover Finds Unexplained Oxygen on Mars
      By Robin George Andrews

# Global Climatic Change on Mars

by Jeffrey S. Kargel and Robert G. Strom

T o those of us who have spent a good part of our lives studying Mars, the newly discovered evidence that extraterrestrial microbes may have once lived in a rock cast off from that planet stirs feelings of awe. But the recent claim also evokes thoughts of Percival Lowell, a well-known American astronomer of the early 20th century, who turned his telescope toward Mars and saw a vast network of canals bordered by vegetation. His suggestion that Mars harbored such lushness had many people believing that the surface of the planet enjoyed conditions not so different from those on Earth. But in the 1960s three Mariner spacecraft flew by Mars and revealed the true harshness of its environment.

Observations from those unmanned probes indicated that Mars has an atmosphere that is thin, cold and dry. This tenuous shroud, composed almost entirely of carbon dioxide, provides less than 1 percent of the surface pressure found at sea level on Earth. The images radioed back during those first fleeting encounters three decades ago were fuzzy and few in number, but they were decidedly more accurate than Lowell's telescopic views. The Mariner cameras showed no canals, no water and no vegetation. They presented only a moonlike surface covered with craters. Sober scientists quickly dismissed any notion that the climate on Mars was sufficiently warm or wet to sustain life.

With its distant orbit—50 percent farther from the sun than Earth—and slim atmospheric blanket, Mars experiences frigid weather conditions. Surface temperatures typically average about −60 degrees Celsius (−76 degrees Fahrenheit) at the equator and can dip to −123 degrees C near the poles. Only the midday sun at tropical latitudes is warm enough to thaw ice on occasion, but any liquid water formed in this way would evaporate almost instantly because of the low atmospheric pressure.

Although the atmosphere holds a small amount of water, and water-ice clouds sometimes develop, most Martian weather involves blowing dust or carbon dioxide. Each winter, for example, a blizzard of frozen carbon dioxide rages over one pole, and a few meters of this dry-ice snow accumulate as previously frozen carbon dioxide evaporates from the opposite polar cap. Yet even on the summer pole, where the sun remains in the sky all day long, temperatures never warm enough to melt frozen water.

Despite the abundant evidence for cold, dry conditions, the impression of Mars as a perpetually freeze-dried world has been steadily giving way since the Mariner probes first reported their findings. Planetary scientists, who continue to examine the voluminous data from both the Mariner and the later Viking missions of the 1970s, now realize that Mars has had a complex climatic history—one that was perhaps punctuated with many relatively warm episodes. At certain times, huge volumes of water flowed freely across the surface of the planet. Before considering what this astonishing fact means for the possibility of life evolving on Mars or the strategy for the next round of Martian exploration, it is instructive to review how this reversal in the way Mars is perceived came about.

## Muddy Recollections

Scrutinizing the Mariner and Viking images obtained from orbit, planetary scientists soon noticed that most old Martian craters (unlike lunar ones) are eroded and that features resembling mudflows occur around almost every large, young crater on Mars. Such muddy "ejecta" probably represent the frozen remnants of a cataclysmic moment in the past when an asteroid or comet collided with the Martian surface, melting a patch of icy permafrost (where water-saturated ground had been frozen) and excavating a large hole that tapped a zone containing liquid water deep underground. By the late 1970s planetologists concluded that a considerable amount of underground ice and water has been present below the Martian surface throughout much of the history of the planet.

Yet not all Martian craters have these muddy flows surrounding them. Smaller craters appear more like their counterparts on the moon, with just streaks of dry ejecta scattered around them. Near the equator of Mars, only craters greater than about four kilometers in diameter display muddy ejecta, but closer to the Martian poles, craters as small as one kilometer across also have relic mudflows. This dependence on latitude arises because the ice-free, surficial layer varies in thickness. This layer extends deeper near the equator (to about 800 meters) than near the poles because the relative warmth of the Martian tropics purges much of the subsurface of frozen water. Hence, near the equator only the impact of bigger objects (that is, those that leave relatively large craters) will burrow down through the upper layer to heat the underlying icy permafrost and release a torrent of mud.

Researchers have since found other indications that a thick substratum of frozen ground exists on Mars. They have also identified evidence that ice once formed on the surface, where it appears to have created characteristic glacial landscapes. These features include bouldery ridges of sediment left by melting glaciers at their margins and meandering lines of sand and gravel deposited beneath glaciers by streams running under the ice (so-called eskers).

Many telltale landforms on Mars resemble frosty sites on Earth. For example, the pitted terrain on Mars corresponds to an earthly equivalent called thermokarst, which forms when the ice contained at shallow levels melts and the ground collapses. The apron-shaped lobes of rocky debris seen on the flanks of some Martian mountains might be rubble-covered glaciers. Or, more likely, they represent "rock glaciers," like the ones that form within the Alaska Range and in the Antarctic Dry Valleys on Earth. These distinctive sloping surfaces result after thousands of freeze-thaw cycles cause the top meter or so of water-soaked ground to creep slowly downhill.

Glacial features and muddy ejecta around craters are not the only examples of water shaping the Martian surface. In some places, sinuous valleys one kilometer wide and many hundreds of kilometers long form large branching networks. Carl Sagan of Cornell University, Victor R. Baker of the University of Arizona and their colleagues suggested in the 1970s that such troughs were created by running water. Other Martian valleys have blunt starting points and short tributaries, characteristics that are typical of erosion by groundwater "sapping." That process, common on Earth, results from the seepage of water from underground springs, which causes the overlying rock and soil to wash away.

Images of Mars also reveal enormous outflow channels etched on the surface. Some of these structures are more than 200 kilometers wide and can stretch for 2,000 kilometers or more. These channels emanate from what is called chaotic terrain, regions of fractured, jumbled rocks that apparently collapsed when groundwater suddenly surged outward. The ensuing floods carved the vast channels, leaving streamlined islands more than 100 kilometers long and gouging cavernous potholes several hundred meters deep. Baker compared the Martian outflow channels to similar, albeit smaller, flood features found on Earth in parts of Oregon and Washington State. Those so-called channeled scablands of the Pacific Northwest formed after a glacier that had dammed a large lake broke open suddenly and caused a catastrophic flood.

The geometry of the Martian outflow channels indicates that water could have flowed along the surface as rapidly as 75 meters per second (170 miles per hour). Michael H. Carr of the U.S. Geological Survey estimates that the vast quantity of water necessary to create these many enormous channels would have been enough to fill a global Martian ocean that was 500 meters deep, although not all this liquid flowed at one time. One source for that great quantity of water may have been a deep lake in Valles Marineris, a region on Mars partly covered with sedimentary layers that appear to be ancient lake deposits. Water could also have gushed from a large reservoir under ice-impregnated permafrost that had been warmed by heat from the interior of the planet.

Why should such an underground accumulation of water suddenly inundate the surface? Scientists are unsure of the exact cause, but this groundwater might have started to flow after the icy permafrost capping it thinned and weakened, perhaps because of a sudden climate warming, volcanism or tectonic uplift. Perhaps a large meteor impact or quake triggered the cataclysmic dousing. Once water broke through to the surface, carbon dioxide from saturated groundwater—a Martian seltzer of sorts—may have erupted in tremendous geysers, further undermining the stability of the saturated underground layers. The result was to produce chaotic terrain and to unleash floods and mudflows of a magnitude that has rarely, if ever, been matched by any earthly deluge.

## An Ocean Away

Some highland areas on Mars contain extensive systems of valleys that drained into sediment-floored depressions. These lowlands were at one time full of water. The largest of these Martian lakes filled two gigantic impact basins called Hellas and Argyre.

But these lakes may not have been the largest bodies of water on the planet. Research groups led by David H. Scott and Kenneth L. Tanaka of the U.S. Geological Survey and by Jeffrey M. Moore of the National Aeronautics and Space Administration Ames Research Center independently concluded that repeated floods from the outflow channels emptied to the north and formed a succession of transient lakes and seas. We have interpreted many features bordering these ancient basins as marking where glaciers once emptied into these deep bodies of water. Tanaka and Moore believe that thick layers of sediment deposited in these seas now stretch across much of the extensive northern plains. According to several estimates, one of the larger of the northern seas on Mars could have displaced the combined volume of the Gulf of Mexico and the Mediterranean Sea.

Yet even that great body of water may not have been the supreme example: there may have been a Mars ocean. As early as 1973 the late Henry Faul of the University of Pennsylvania raised this intriguing possibility in a paper he romantically entitled "The Cliff of Nix Olympica." Understandably, given the paucity of observations then available, the paper was never accepted for publication. But during the past decade, other researchers, working with information acquired during the Viking missions, have revived Faul's idea.

For instance, in 1989 Timothy J. Parker and his colleagues at the Jet Propulsion Laboratory in Pasadena, Calif., again proposed a northern ocean (arguing that many features in the northern plains looked as if they had resulted from coastal erosion). To enhance prospects for publication, however, they deliberately obscured the provocative thrust of their work with the mundane title "Transitional Morphology in the West Deuteronilus Mensae Region of Mars: Implications for Modification of the Lowland/Upland Boundary." In a subsequent paper, these researchers ventured a more direct title to convey their ideas: "Coastal Geomorphology of the Martian Northern Plains." Motivated in part by such work, Baker and several colleagues (including us) named this hypothetical northern ocean Oceanus Borealis. We calculated that it was possibly four times as large as the Arctic Ocean on Earth, and we proposed a scenario for the actions of the water cycle on Mars that could have accounted for it.

Whereas most planetary scientists now agree that large bodies of water formed repeatedly in the northern plains on Mars, many do not accept that there was ever a true ocean there. Some envision that only a vast, muddy slurry, or mud ocean, existed. In any case, it is clear that huge amounts of water once flowed over the surface of Mars. Yet the fate of that water remains unknown. Some of it may have percolated into the subsurface and frozen in permafrost. Some may have frozen in place and might now stretch across much of the floor of the northern plains, hidden by a mantle of dust and sand. Some water may simply have evaporated, to be later lost to space or deposited as snow at the poles.

## Trust the Old Salts

Although images of the landforms left by ancient glaciers, river valleys, lakes and seas are strong testament that Mars was once rich in water, evidence comes from other sources as well. Earth-based spectroscopic measurements of Mars reveal the presence of clay minerals. Even more directly, the two landers that set down on the surface during the Viking program analyzed Martian soil and found that it probably contains 10 to 20 percent salts. Martian rocks, like those on Earth, react to form salt and clay minerals when exposed to water. But such chemical weathering probably cannot occur under the cold and dry conditions that now reign on Mars.

Some scientists have also studied Martian rocks found here on Earth. These rare samples of the Martian surface were blasted into space by the impact of an asteroid or comet and later fell to Earth as meteorites. Allan H. Treiman of the Lunar and Planetary Institute in Houston and James L. Gooding of the NASA Johnson Space Center have shown in the past several years that minerals in some of these so-called SNC meteorites were chemically altered by cool, salty water, whereas others were affected by warmer hydrothermal solutions. Their conclusions imply that Mars once had a relatively warm, wet climate and may have had hot springs. Just perhaps, conditions were right for life.

That possibility inspired David S. McKay of the NASA Johnson Space Center and his colleagues to examine an SNC meteorite for signs of ancient Martian life. Although their conclusion that fossil microbes are present is open to debate (and a vigorous one is indeed going on), the composition of the rock they studied—with fractures filled by minerals that probably precipitated from an aqueous solution—indicated that conditions on Mars a few billion years ago would have been compatible with the existence of life.

In agreement with this assessment, many atmospheric physicists had already concluded that Mars has lost immense quantities of water vapor to space over time. Their theoretical calculations are in good accord with measurements made by various Soviet space probes that showed oxygen and hydrogen atoms (derived from breakdown of atmospheric water exposed to sunlight) streaming away from Mars. The continuous loss of these elements implies that Mars must once have had all the water needed to fill an Oceanus Borealis.

But water was not the only substance lost. Recently David M. Kass and Yuk L. Yung of the California Institute of Technology examined the evolution of carbon dioxide—a potent greenhouse gas—in the atmosphere of Mars. They found that over time an enormous quantity of carbon dioxide has escaped to space. That amount of gaseous carbon dioxide would have constituted a thick Martian atmosphere with three times the pressure found at the surface of Earth. The greenhouse effect from that gas would have been sufficient to warm most of the surface of Mars above the freezing point of water. Thus, from this perspective, too, it seems quite plausible that the climate on Mars once was much warmer and wetter than it is today.

Yet many questions remain about how water might have arranged itself on the surface of Mars: Was there actually an ocean? Did water shift rapidly between different reservoirs? When and for how long was Mars wet? Although the absolute timing of these events remains unknown, most researchers believe that water sculpted the surface of Mars at many intervals throughout the history of the planet. The constant loss of water and carbon dioxide from the atmosphere suggests that early epochs on Mars (that is, billions of years ago) may have been especially warm and wet. But some balmy periods may also have been relatively recent: Timothy D. Swindle of the University of Arizona and his colleagues studied minerals in an SNC meteorite created by aqueous alteration and determined that they formed 300 million years ago—a long time by human standards but only a few percent of the age of the 4.6-billion-year-old solar system. Their result was, however, accompanied by a considerable degree of uncertainty.

The duration of the wet periods on Mars is also difficult to gauge exactly. If the eroded Martian landscapes formed under conditions typical of terrestrial glacial environments, more than a few thousand but less than about a million years of warm, wet climate were required. Had these conditions endured substantially longer, erosion would have presumably erased all but traces of a few impact craters, just as it does on Earth.

## A Mars Probe Parade

There are nine scientific programs to explore Mars now in preparation or on the drawing board, and three of these unmanned missions will be launched this month and next. The first probe—Mars Global Surveyor—is scheduled to blast off on

November 5. During the summer of 1997 the Surveyor craft will go into orbit around Mars, a vantage from which it will be able to map the surface in fine detail.

Less than two weeks after the launch of Surveyor, the international Mars '96 mission will commence. Russia, in collaboration with Germany, France, Finland and several other nations, is sending a small scientific armada: one spacecraft will enter into orbit around Mars, two landing craft will gently touch down, and two "penetrators" will bury themselves deeply in the Martian soil.

Early in December the National Aeronautics and Space Administration will launch its second probe of this year, Mars Pathfinder. Seven months later Pathfinder will set down on the surface within the mouth of an ancient outwash channel. This event will occur on July 4, which will be 21 years to the day after Viking 1 settled onto the surface of the red planet. Once safely perched on the Martian surface, Pathfinder will release a small six-wheeled vehicle to explore the terrain immediately around the touchdown point.

Within a decade, scientists will send at least four additional orbiting spacecraft and five more surface probes to examine Mars. Although the U.S. strategy for the exploration originally called for a sample return mission to be carried out in 2005, the recent discovery of evidence that microscopic life-forms may have existed on Mars has prompted NASA to consider accelerating that schedule.

Such a mission to bring Martian rocks back to Earth, though the most scientifically exciting, is also the most technically daunting of all the programs yet planned. The probe will be able to carry sufficient quantities of hydrogen (a conveniently light element) to fuel the return trip, but the spacecraft might have to restock with the heavier oxygen that it needs to burn this hydrogen during the ride home. To solve that problem, the spacecraft may have to generate a supply of oxygen on the surface of Mars by breaking down carbon dioxide, a substance that is, fortunately, available in copious amounts in the Martian atmosphere.

—J.S.K. and R.G.S.

This limitation does not apply to the earliest history of the planet, billions of years ago, before the craters now visible had formed. A young Mars may well have had vigorous erosion smoothing its face. But eventually, as the planet slipped toward middle age, its visage became cold, dry and pockmarked. Only scattered intervals of warmth have since rejuvenated the surface of the planet in certain regions. Yet the mechanism that causes Mars to switch between mild and frigid regimes remains largely mysterious. Scientists can now venture only crude explanations for how these climate changes might have occurred.

## Turning on the Heat

One hypothesis involves shifts in obliquity, the tilt of the spin axis from its ideal position, perpendicular to the orbital plane. Mars, like Earth, is now canted by about 24 degrees, and that tilt changes regularly over time. Jihad Touma and Jack L. Wisdom of the Massachusetts Institute of Technology discovered in 1993 that, for Mars, the tilt can also change abruptly. Excursions of the tilt axis through a range of as much as 60 degrees may recur sporadically every 10 million years or so. In addition, the orientation of the tilt axis and the shape of the orbit that Mars follows both change cyclically with time.

These celestial machinations, particularly the tendency of the spin axis to tilt far over, can cause seasonal temperature extremes. Even with a thin atmosphere such as the one that exists today, summer temperatures at middle and high Martian latitudes during periods with large obliquity could have climbed above freezing for weeks on end, and Martian winters would have been even harsher than they are currently.

But with sufficient summer warming of one pole, the atmosphere may have changed drastically. Releases of gas from the warmed polar cap, from seltzer groundwater or from carbon dioxide–rich permafrost may have thickened the atmosphere sufficiently to create a temporary greenhouse climate. Water could then have existed on the surface. Aqueous chemical reactions during such warm periods would in turn form salts and carbonate rocks. That process would slowly draw carbon dioxide from the atmosphere, thereby reducing the greenhouse effect. A return to moderate levels of obliquity might further cool the planet and precipitate dry-ice snow, thinning the atmosphere even more and returning Mars to its normal, frigid state.

This theory of climatic change needs to be tested, but new observations and fresh insights will undoubtedly come from a decade-long series of unpiloted spacecraft that will next visit Mars. The expeditions begin this month with the launch of American and Russian probes. This program of exploration had been slated to conclude in 2005 with the return of Martian rocks. But the discovery of what may be fossil microbes in an SNC meteorite has sparked thoughts of obtaining Martian samples sooner so that scientists can better evaluate whether microorganisms existed on Mars several billion years ago—or even more recently.

The American spacecraft soon to be under way include Mars Pathfinder and Mars Global Surveyor. Pathfinder will land on a bouldery plain of an outflow channel that once fed an ancient sea. Although not equipped to test directly for signs of life, this lander will release a small roving vehicle to explore the local environs. Surveyor will take pictures from orbit that can resolve features that are just a few meters across. Measurements from this orbiter will also allow scientists to make detailed topographic maps and to search for icy deposits as well as new evidence of ancient glaciers, lakes and rivers. Information gathered by these next missions should give scientists a clearer picture of what Mars looked like during its last episode of warmer climate, perhaps 300 million years in the past.

By 300 million years ago on Earth, amphibians evolved from fish had crawled out of the sea and inhabited swampy coastlines. Might other complex creatures have flourished simultaneously along Martian shores? The basic conditions for life may have existed for a million years late in Martian history—perhaps much longer during an earlier period. Were these intervals conducive for organisms to evolve into forms that could survive the dramatic changes in climate?

Could Martian organisms still survive today in underground hot springs? The next decade of concentrated exploration may provide the definitive answers, which, if positive, would mark an intellectual leap as great as any in human history.

## Referenced

Ancient Oceans, Ice Sheets and the Hydrological Cycle on Mars. V. R. Baker, R. G. Strom, V. C. Gulick, J. S. Kargel, G. Komatsu and V. S. Kale in *Nature*, Vol. 352, pages 589–594; August 15, 1991.

Ancient Glaciation on Mars. J. S. Kargel and R. G. Strom in *Geology*, Vol. 20, No. 1, pages 3–7; January 1992.

The Ice Ages of Mars. J. S. Kargel and R. G. Strom in *Astronomy*, Vol. 20, No. 12, pages 40–45; December 1992.

Coastal Geomorphology of the Martian Northern Plains. T. J. Parker, D. S. Gorsline, R. S. Saunders, D. C. Pieri and D. M. Schneeberger in *Journal of Geophysical Research E (Planets)*, Vol. 98, No. 6, pages 11061–11078; June 25, 1993.

## About the Authors

*Jeffrey S. Kargel and Robert G. Strom have worked together on various projects in planetary science for over a decade. Kargel met Strom soon after beginning graduate studies at the University of Arizona, where he received a doctorate in planetary sciences in 1990. Kargel remained at the University of Arizona's Lunar and Planetary Science Laboratory for two years doing postdoctoral research on the icy moons of the outer solar system and then joined the U.S. Geological Survey's astrogeology group in Flagstaff. Strom began his career working as a petroleum geologist, but he became involved in lunar exploration efforts during the 1960s and joined the faculty of the University of Arizona, where he continues to teach and conduct research. He has participated on National Aeronautics and Space Administration science teams assembled for the Apollo program, for the Mariner missions to Venus and Mercury, and for the Voyager missions to outer solar system.*

# The Distant Shores of Mars

By Caleb A. Scharf

Once upon a time it seems that Mars had oceans. But the exact appearance of these bodies of surface water, their sizes and distribution is a matter of intense debate. Most evidence points towards the deep past, some 4 billion years ago as the age when Mars could have held marine environments. Since then the red planet may have been largely cold and arid, with only the occasional shift of climate conditions.

For many geoscientists, some of the most compelling evidence of those old, old watery bodies comes from the topographic and mineralogical signs of ancient shorelines. These so-called "contacts" are seen as geological boundaries, especially in the northern plains of Mars. Crossing thousands of kilometers they are associated with past oceanic basins whose rather romantic names, like Arabia and Deuteronilus, belie their current state of extinction.

But these wiggly contact lines are not without controversy. For one thing, they don't seem to quite follow a so-called equipotential surface. This is an imaginary surface defined by the local gravitational acceleration–a surefire way to determine how an ocean settles against the gnarly topography of a rocky planet. But on a spinning planet, centripetal acceleration counters gravitational acceleration, so the equipotential surfaces depend to a large degree on where the spin axis of a planet is in relation to its geographic features. Shift the spin axis and you also shift the equator, where planetary spin tends to bulge everything outwards.

It gets even more complicated when there's lots of liquid water. A big ocean loads the planetary crust and alters the mass distribution on a world. Together with geophysical building (like large volcanic upwellings) a planet, much like a spinning top, can wobble as its surface mass shifts around. On Mars it seems likely that a fair amount of True Polar Wander (or TPW) may have happened as a result. TPW means that the spin poles literally shift relative to geography. On early Mars there may have been as much as 30-60 degrees of TPW. That's like having the geographic North pole on Earth move from the Arctic to as far away as Cairo in Egypt. The resulting changes in centripetal acceleration will alter where shorelines settle.

But, as a new work by Citron, Manga, & Hemingway in *Nature* explains, on Mars this raises some questions. One of the biggest, baddest volcanic features on Mars is the Tharsis volcanic province–a vast plateau containing some of the largest shield volcanoes in the solar system. When the Tharsis region formed, starting about 3.7 billion years ago, it would be possible for later-forming oceans to drive the needed TPW to explain their shoreline locations. Except, for this to all work Tharsis would have had to be a long way from the equator, and other evidence suggests that it was very close to the equator; where its massive bulk would in effect prevent any later TPW due to new oceans.

The authors propose a solution: have some of the oceans form early, 4 billion years ago and before Tharsis. Then, as the volcanic structure pushed its way onto the surface of Mars, like a nasty set of pimples, it would have changed the topography and caused its own TPW. The result would be a set of shorelines that make more sense. Older oceans (like Arabia) would be less anomalous, and later oceans (like Deuteronilus at about 3.6 billion years ago) would still fit the post-Tharsis landscape.

This timing also means that the size and evolution of oceans on early Mars could be tightly related to huge volcanic events—either reducing the amount of water or perhaps increasing it as outgassed material condensed.

In other words, the shorelines on Mars are probably giving us critical insight to when these ancient oceans formed and existed. That information, if it can be supported by other data on ages and geophysical events, helps us build a more complete picture of the environment on Mars four billion years ago. A time when it is conceivable that life was emerging for the first time in the solar system.

*The views expressed are those of the author(s) and are not necessarily those of* Scientific American.

## About the Author

*Caleb A. Scharf is director of astrobiology at Columbia University. He is author and co-author of more than 100 scientific research articles in astronomy and astrophysics. His work has been featured in publications such as* New Scientist, Scientific American, Science News, Cosmos Magazine, Physics Today *and* National Geographic. *For many years he wrote the Life, Unbounded blog for* Scientific American.

# Dust Bowl Mars

By Caleb A. Scharf

Mars is a very dusty world. Having spent most of the past few billions of years in an extremely dry and frigid state its rocks just keep on eroding to tiny particles. And with sizes as small as individual talcum powder grains (about 3 microns) and a lower surface gravity than Earth, even the thin martian atmosphere can loft these particles high into the sky.

Most of the time the lofting and rearranging of dust is done by the dust devils that spin across the planetary surface. At any given moment on Mars there are an estimated 10,000 or so active dust devils. Imaging data can reveal the tracks left by some of these on the martian landscape, and barometric data from landers also provides clues to their occurrence rates. During the course of a single martian day there may be several million of these swirling dervishes–each popping up for a few minutes at a time.

Not only do they maintain a dust load in the atmosphere (where the particles help warm the air and influences global climate), they also rearrange the dust. It's a bit like having a vast army of rather incompetent cleaners, siphoning up dust from one place and simply depositing it somewhere else. Unlike Earth, with a wet biosphere that washes dust from the atmosphere and helps bind rock particles into soil and sediments, dust on Mars is more or less eternal.

Although not fully understood, it also seems likely that the movement of dust grains generates electrical potentials–high enough perhaps for lightning-like discharges, and certainly enough to make the dust extra sticky for any robotic or human exploration.

But dust devils are typically highly localized phenomena. Mars also experiences dust storms on much grander scales. During the southern spring and summer on Mars, coinciding with the closest approach to the Sun in the elliptical martian orbit, storms are common. At this distance there is 45 percent more solar radiation hitting Mars than at its farthest from the Sun.

There's a double-barreled driver for these seasonal storms: The atmosphere warms up and winds get stronger, driven by greater contrasts in surface temperature. And frozen carbon dioxide on the southern polar cap sublimates, raising the global atmospheric pressure. A thicker atmosphere means a longer hang time for dust particles, and storms can loft material up to over 60 kilometers altitude.

To add insult to planetary injury, it seems possible that dust storms can contribute to the drying out of Mars. Grains can carry water molecules to high enough altitudes that sunlight breaks molecular bonds, hydrogen escapes to space and those water molecules can never reform.

Although they're large these seasonal storms generally remain confined to a particular geographical area. For example, the great Hellas Basin in the south. But about every 3 martian years (about 5.5 Earth years) they can explode into global events–in other words a roughly one-in-three probability in a given year. Even though the windspeeds are never shocking by Earth standards, perhaps hitting 60 miles an hour (96 km an hour), the entire planet can become enshrouded by dust in just days.

As I write this, Mars is in the midst of just such a global storm. The rovers Curiosity and Opportunity are having to sit through it–a much bigger challenge for the solar-powered Opportunity than the radioisotope-powered Curiosity. Indeed, Curiosity can keep up its exploration program beneath the darkened skies.

Over the years we've seen many examples of these global events. Perhaps the most memorable one was actually the first seen up-close. When Mariner 9 became the first probe to orbit another planet in 1971 it happened to arrive precisely when Mars was utterly blanketed in a dust storm. I wrote about this a while back, and how the mission science had to be put on hold for two months until the storm cleared.

Another particularly huge storm took place in 2001, this time seen by NASA's Mars Global Surveyor. During this one, while the lower to middle atmosphere actually warmed up by about 40 Kelvin, the planet's surface temperature plunged by as much as 20 Kelvin. All the dust blocked sunlight from warming the ground.

That surface cooling might be extremely challenging for robots or humans on the surface of Mars, but it also presages the end of the storm itself. A cooler surface generates less of the lofting winds, and so by the time the storm's presence has chilled the ground it's pretty much doomed itself.

Why do these global storms spring up on Mars in the first place? Well, we don't really understand the precise mechanism that makes some storms so much bigger than others. But each time we get to witness one we can gather more data to probe this ancient, harsh, and extraordinarily beautiful world.

*The views expressed are those of the author(s) and are not necessarily those of Scientific American.*

## About the Author

*Caleb A. Scharf is director of astrobiology at Columbia University. He is author and co-author of more than 100 scientific research articles in astronomy and astrophysics. His work has been featured in publications such as* New Scientist, Scientific American, Science News, Cosmos Magazine, Physics Today *and* National Geographic. *For many years he wrote the* Life, Unbounded *blog for* Scientific American.

# NASA's Curiosity Rover Finds Unexplained Oxygen on Mars

By Robin George Andrews

NASA's Curiosity rover, for three Martian years—nearly six years to us Earthlings—has been sniffing the air above Mars' Gale Crater, its near-equatorial exploration site. Using its Sample Analysis at Mars (SAM) portable chemistry lab, the rover has ascertained not only what the surface atmosphere is made of, but also how its gases change with the seasons.

Many of Mars' gases "are very well behaved," says Melissa Trainer, a planetary scientist at NASA and a team member on the SAM experiment. One, however, appears to be behaving in a decidedly unexpected and altogether bizarre manner: oxygen.

Scientists have long known that carbon dioxide on Mars, which makes up 95 percent of the planet's atmosphere, freezes out over the poles in winter, and sublimates back into a gas in summer. In the thin air around Gale Crater, Curiosity's measurements have shown tiny amounts of inert argon and nitrogen periodically rising and falling as expected, due to this seasonal cycling of carbon dioxide.

Curiosity's instruments also registered atmospheric oxygen rising and falling at similar times but in amounts that defy easy explanation. There was far more of it during the spring and summer, and less of it in the winter, than the seasonal whooshing back and forth of other gases would predict.

That suggests something is making or unleashing stores of oxygen in the warmer months and trapping or swallowing it up during frigid ones. It could be a geological, chemical, atmospheric or, perhaps even a biological process, but right now, no one has the foggiest as to what the culprit actually is. And although the oxygen's trampolining certainly appears to be a local feature, it might be a regional or even global peculiarity.

François Forget, a planetary scientist at the French National Center for Scientific Research, says that this finding is surprising, weird and mysterious. Jon Telling, a geochemist and geomicrobiologist at Newcastle University, says he and other experts are understandably "flummoxed."

An unanticipated challenge has suddenly been laid out before the scientific community. It is unclear when, or even if, the case of the overzealous oxygen will be cracked. Already, says Paul Niles, a planetary geologist and analytical geochemist at NASA, it is abundantly clear that "Mars is a lot more alien than we thought."

## Curiosity Killed the Stats

In situ measurements of the pressure, temperature and composition of Mars' atmosphere date back nearly a half century, from the Viking landers in the 1970s through to the Spirit, Opportunity and now Curiosity rovers. Curiosity's SAM suite, however, has painstakingly tracked how Martian atmospheric gas amounts change through the seasons, thereby providing scientists with a game-changing, precise chronicle of the planet's atmosphere.

Oxygen's too-high spikes and too-low nadirs during the warmer and colder months, respectively, came as a shock. Curiosity's scientists could conceive of only two possibilities: either a mysterious creator and destroyer of oxygen existed on Mars that scientists were unaware of, or the measurements were wrong. Trainer, lead author of the study reporting the discovery in the *Journal of Geophysical Research: Planets*, emphasizes that this detection and analysis took many years, with all possible false positive triggers ruled out.

"I think they've done their due diligence," Niles says. Plenty can go wrong with these interplanetary science experiments, from equipment malfunctions to contamination. Regardless, he says, "I don't see any reason to have any doubt in the oxygen measurements."

"I hope it's real," Forget says, because an extraterrestrial oxygen enigma is far more fun than a glitch.

A true enigma would force researchers to go back to basics, says Manish Patel, a planetary scientist at the Open University. "We must first interrogate our understanding of the known processes for creating oxygen, before we invoke any new, or controversial, processes."

Trainer and her colleagues did just that. But they still came up short. Solar radiation could be breaking up oxygen molecules and blowing them away into space, but this process appears to be too slow and inefficient to account for the seasonal dips seen by Curiosity. Perhaps carbon dioxide's slow breakdown in the atmosphere could have released oxygen, causing a summertime spike—but again, this process would take too long to produce the observed peaks.

Martian soil is rich in oxygen-containing hydrogen peroxide and perchlorates. The Viking landers demonstrated that warm, damp air could free this oxygen, but those conditions do not prevail across enough of the planet—let alone Gale Crater—to suffice for the SAM data. Soil bombardment by ionizing radiation from cosmic rays and solar storms might do the trick, but is estimated to require a million years to create the oxygen peak seen during one solitary spring.

We simply do not know enough about Mars to get a grip on this particular puzzle, says Niles. So much about its chemistry—how gases are transported above and within the planet, what sources and sinks they may have—remains deeply uncertain. For all we know, he says, events in Mars' past could have conspired to lock away vast amounts of oxygen belowground, which is now, for some reason, surging back into the atmosphere.

If the answer is not to be found in Mars' lifeless air and rocks, could some cryptic, alien form of biology be to blame? On Earth, photosynthesis and respiration by living things cause tiny fluctuations in our planet's otherwise steady oxygen concentration. We shouldn't expect this on Mars, though. "That's far out," Telling says: Mars appears too inhospitable for a critical mass of life capable of sustaining either process. "It's almost certainly going to be a nonbiological chemical reaction."

Trainer herself does not rule out a biological explanation, but nevertheless underscores its unlikeliness. "People in the community like to say that it will be the explanation of last resort, because that would be so monumental," she says. There are abiotic mechanisms aplenty, both known and unknown, to rule out first before leaping to any more sensational claims.

## Riding the Methane Rollercoaster

This oxygen conundrum is reminiscent of Mars' mischievous methane, another of the Red Planet's long-standing mystery. Although Martian air contains a persistent low background level of methane, for years multiple independent groups of scientists have claimed detections of dramatic, unpredictable spikes in the gas' atmospheric abundance. Curiosity spotted one such spike in 2013, and another substantially greater one in 2019. Puzzlingly, many ground-based methane detections have not been corroborated by atmosphere-probing spacecraft high above the Martian surface, including ESA's Trace Gas Orbiter and Mars Express.

Methane has a wide range of sources and sinks on Earth. Some are geological, but many are biological. On Mars, airborne methane should break down quickly, so any spikes are presumed to have been generated shortly before a detection is made; this fact has fueled speculation over an extant Martian microbial progenitor as the cause of Curiosity's observed spikes. But as with oxygen, "methane is completely puzzling as well," Forget says. Scientists can say little about it with any certainty, including whether it crops up on a local, regional or global scale, and why.

If Mars' methane spikes are genuine, and caused by some as-yet-unknown chemical process, scientists posit this should have knock-on effects for other gases in the atmosphere—but nothing of the sort has ever been observed. Until now, that is: Curiosity's SAM readings suggest that oxygen levels, across the seasons, sometimes rise and fall with Mars' methane concentrations.

"It's certainly not a perfect match," Trainer says; for each gas, the timings and extremities of the spikes and troughs diverge, which suggests both gases are controlled by different combinations of processes. If, however, the implied imperfectly synchronized dance between the two gases is real, then understanding one's behavior may help us comprehend the other.

With so many questions in hand, where do we go from here? Sniffing more of the air down at Mars' surface with SAM would always be welcome, Trainer says; that data can be fed into models and laboratory experiments that may unravel the mystery of Mars' manic oxygen.

Curiosity, though, is only huffing gas in one single area, so its data are ill-suited for confirming whether this oxygen roller-coaster is a local or global occurrence, says Patel. The Trace Gas Orbiter, however, could be a big help. "I will really bet a lot that if this oxygen variation is real, it has to be quite global," says Forget—and this orbiter is well placed to determine that.

It is too early to predict if this will be a colossal or miniature phenomenon, one with a rudimentary explanation or a far more revolutionary root. At present, Trainer says, all we can confidently say about Mars' wild oxygen levels is that "we're pulling on all the current understanding we have and saying, gosh, it just doesn't add up."

## About the Author

*Robin George Andrews is a volcanologist, author and science writer based in London. His first book,* Super Volcanoes: What They Reveal about Earth and the Worlds Beyond, *was published in November 2021.*

# GLOSSARY

**arid** Dry or low in precipitation.

**caldera** A circular crater resulting from a volcanic eruption.

**conjecture** A theory or opinion arrived at with limited data.

**corroborate** To provide evidence confirming another argument or scientific conclusion.

**ejecta** Materials that are launched as a result of a volcanic eruption or meteor collision

**friable** Easily pulverized or crumbled.

**igneous** A category of rock defined by volcanic origin in lava drawn from a planet's mantle.

**lander** A spacecraft designed to land on the surface of a planet or moon; not to be confused with rover.

**mantle** The layer between a planet's crust and core.

**orbiter** A spacecraft designed to observe a planet from its orbit only.

**organic compound** A chemical compound containing carbon and often appearing in living organisms.

**permafrost** A layer of soil that remains below freezing for long periods of time.

**planetary protection** Policies set by international space agencies for the prevention of contamination of celestial bodies by Earth-based microbes.

**reconnaissance** The act of gathering information.

**regolith** Deposits of loose rocks, dust, and other materials covering a layer of bedrock.

**rover** A vehicle designed to explore the surface of a planet or moon.

**signatory**  A participant in an agreement, such as a country to an international treaty.

**spectrometer**  A device for measuring and analyzing a spectrum of light emitted during a physical process; commonly used in many branches of space research.

**sublimation**  The transition of a substance from solid to gas state without first melting to liquid.

**tectonic**  The activity and movement of elements of a planet's crust.

**terraforming**  The proposed transformation of a planet to make it Earth-like and habitable for human life.

# FURTHER INFORMATION

Andrews, Robin George. "Rocks, Rockets and Robots: The Plan to Bring Mars Down to Earth." *Scientific American*, February 6, 2020, https://www.scientificamerican.com/article/rocks-rockets-and-robots-the-plan-to-bring-mars-down-to-earth1/.

Limoli, Charles L. "Could Radiation Be a Deal Breaker for Mars Missions?" *Scientific American*, February 1, 2017, https://www.scientificamerican.com/article/could-radiation-be-a-deal-breaker-for-mars-missions/.

Moskowitz, Clara. "Looking for Life on Mars: Viking Experiment Team Member Reflects on Divisive Findings." *Scientific American*, April 2, 2019, https://www.scientificamerican.com/article/looking-for-life-on-mars-viking-experiment-team-member-reflects-on-divisive-findings/.

Moskowitz, Clara. "Winter in the Antarctic Shows What It Will Take to Live on Mars." *Scientific American*, February 13, 2014, https://www.scientificamerican.com/article/mars-analogue-missions-concordia/.

Murray, Bruce C., and James A. Westphal. "Infrared Astronomy." *Scientific American*, August 1965, https://www.scientificamerican.com/article/infrared-astronomy/.

NASA. "Mars Persistance Rover Blog." https://mars.nasa.gov/mars2020/mission/status/.

NASA. "Moon to Mars." https://www.nasa.gov/topics/moon-to-mars.

The Planetary Society. "Planetary Protection: How to Explore Mars and Other Worlds Responsibly." https://www.planetary.org/articles/planetary-protection-explore-responsibly.

# CITATIONS

1.1 Skiing to Mars: The Original Rovers by Caleb A. Scharf (July 23, 2012); 1.2 Mars From Mariner 9 by Bruce C. Murray (January 1973); 1.3 The Great Martian Storm of '71 by Caleb A. Scharf (October 21, 2013); 1.4 The Mars Pathfinder Mission by Matthew P. Golombek (July 1998); 1.5 A New Way to Reach Mars Safely, Anytime, and on the Cheap by Adam Hadhazy (December 22, 2014); 1.6 China Lands Tianwen-1 Rover on Mars in Major First for the Country by Jonathan O'Callaghan (May 14, 2021); 2.1 Human Missions to Mars Will Look Completely Different from *The Martian* by Lee Billings (October 2, 2015); 2.2 Is "Protecting" Mars from Contamination a Half-Baked Idea? by Michael J. Battaglia (November 6, 2015); 2.3 Can Mars Be Terraformed? by Christopher Edwards and Bruce Jakosky (August 27, 2018); 2.4 Aerogel Mars by Caleb A. Scharf (October 14, 2019); 2.5 Surviving Mars by Caleb A. Scharf (January 27, 2020); 2.6 How to Grow Vegetables on Mars by Edward Guinan, Scott Engle, and Alicia Eglin (May 10, 2020); 3.1 Water Flows on Mars Today, NASA Announces by Clara Moskowitz (September 28, 2015); 3.2 Searching for Life in Martian Water Will Be Very, Very Tricky by Lee Billings (September 28, 2015); 3.3 The Search for Life on Mars Is About to Get Weird by Leonard David (May 9, 2017); 3.4 Curiosity Rover Uncovers Long-Sought Organic Materials on Martian Surface by Adam Mann (June 7, 2018); 3.5 Deep Within Mars, Liquid Water Offers Hope for Life by Lee Billings (July 25, 2018); 3.6 I'm Convinced We Found Evidence of Life on Mars in the 1970s by Gilbert V. Levin (October 10, 2019); 3.7 Until Recently, People Accepted the 'Fact' of Aliens in the Solar System by Caleb A. Scharf (February 21, 2021); 4.1 The Many Faces of Mars by Philip R. Christensen (July 2005); 4.2 Data Deluge: Texas Flood Canyon Offers Test of Hydrology Theories for Earth and Mars by John Matson (July 21, 2010); 4.3 I Can Tell You About Mars by David Bressan (September 6, 2012); 4.4 Martian Mile-High Mounds Mystery: The Answer Is Blowing in the Wind by Shannon Hall (April 6, 2016); 4.5 Water on Mars May Be Trapped in the Planet's Crust, Not Lost to Space by Jonathan O'Callaghan (March 18, 2021); 5.1 Global Climatic Change on Mars by Jeffrey S. Kargel and Robert G. Strom (November 1996); 5.2 The Distant Shores of Mars by Caleb A. Scharf (March 27, 2018); 5.3 Dust Bowl Mars by Caleb A. Scharf (July 10, 2018); 5.4 NASA'S Curiosity Rover Finds Unexplained Oxygen on Mars by Robin George Andrews (November 20, 2019).

*Each author biography was accurate at the time the article was originally published.*

# INDEX

## A

Andrews, Robin George, 150–154

## B

Battaglia, Michael J., 54–57
Billings, Lee, 50–53, 77–80, 92–96
Bressan, David, 121–122

## C

Christensen, Philip R., 107–117
climate/weather, 6, 22, 35, 67, 70, 84–85, 114, 116, 132–154
craters, 9, 11, 18, 21, 24, 27, 30–31, 33, 54, 77–79, 83, 87, 89, 108, 110–113, 121–125, 130, 132–134, 139, 141, 150, 152

## D

David, Leonard, 81–86
dust, 14–15, 17, 19, 24, 27–29, 34, 36–38, 50, 90, 92, 110, 113, 129, 132, 137, 147–149

## E

Edwards, Christopher, 58–60
Eglin, Alicia, 69–71

## E

Engle, Scott, 69–71
European Space Agency (ESA), 46, 48, 58, 90, 92, 111, 153–154

## G

Golombek, Matthew P., 30–39
Guinan, Edward, 69–71

## H

Hadhazy, Adam, 40–44
Hall, Shannon, 124–126

## J

Jakosky, Bruce, 58–60

## K

Kargel, Jeffrey S., 132–143

## L

Levin, Gilbert V., 97–101
life, 6, 13, 24, 30, 32, 52, 54–63, 69–70, 74, 76–105, 108, 116, 119, 129, 132–133, 138, 140, 142–143, 145, 152–153

## M

Mann, Adam, 87–91
Matson, John, 118–120
Moskowitz, Clara, 74–76
Murray, Bruce C., 11–26, 28

# N

NASA, 12, 40–41, 43–45, 48,
51–55, 58, 69–70, 75–76,
87, 90, 129, 136, 138
NASA missions
Mars Global Surveyor, 28,
39, 109, 121, 139–140,
142, 148
Mars Pathfinder, 8, 30–39,
50, 99, 140, 142
Viking, 9, 25–26, 28, 31–33,
35–38, 46–47, 56, 79,
88, 97, 99–101, 121,
124, 133, 136–137, 140,
152
NASA rovers
Curiosity, 8–9, 47, 54–55,
87–89, 99–100, 122,
148, 150–154
Opportunity, 8, 108–110,
113, 116, 121–122, 148,
151
Perseverance, 45, 47, 130
Sojourner, 8, 31–33, 50, 142
Spirit, 8, 108–109, 113, 151
NASA spacecraft
Mariner 4, 11, 13, 103–104
Mariner 6, 11, 13, 18, 27
Mariner 7, 11, 13–14,
19–20, 27
Mariner 8, 14
Mariner 9, 11–12, 14–15,
19–21, 24–29, 148
Mars Odyssey, 112, 115, 128

Mars Reconnaissance Orbiter
(MRO), 74, 95, 128
MAVEN, 127, 129

# O

O'Callaghan, Jonathan, 45–48,
127–130

# P

planetary protection, 52–57,
61–62, 76–79, 83, 86, 96

# S

Scharf, Caleb A., 8–10, 27–29,
61–68, 102–105, 144–149
Strom, Robert G., 132–143

# V

volcano, 11–12, 15–17, 21,
23, 28, 34–35, 54, 78, 95,
107–109, 111–112, 114,
116, 121, 124–125, 128–
129, 135–136, 144–145

# W

water, 6, 12–13, 16, 18–21,
23, 25, 30–31, 33–36, 38,
47, 50–52, 54–55, 58–59,
61–62, 65–67, 70, 74–79,
82–83, 86–87, 90, 92–96,
107–110 113–116, 119,
122, 125, 127–130, 132–
139, 141–142, 144–145,
148